It is

Step out of condemnation and into the completed work of Christ

Eddie Snipes

A book by
Exchanged Life Discipleship

ISBN 978-1493520749

Published by GES Book Publishing
Carrollton, GA

Copyright © 2013 by Eddie Snipes, Exchanged Life Discipleship, and GES Book Publishing

http://www.exchangedlife.com

All rights reserved. No part of this book may be reproduced in any form or by any electronic or mechanical means including information storage and retrieval systems, without permission in writing from the author. The only exception is by a reviewer, who may quote short excerpts in a review.

Contact the author by visiting http://www.eddiesnipes.com or http://www.exchangedlife.com

Unless otherwise stated, the scripture in this book have been taken from the New King James Version. Copyright © 1982 by Thomas Nelson, Inc. Used by permission. All rights reserved.

Picture Credits
Front cover photo(s) purchased at:
http://www.dreamstime.com

Table of Contents

- Grace is a Verb 5
  - Discussion Questions: 13
- Grasping Grace 14
  - Discussion Questions 22
- Assurance of Grace 23
  - Discussion Questions 30
- Transformation of Grace 32
  - New Creation 35
  - Did the Law come to an end? 37
  - Discussion Questions 40
- Understanding Complete Forgiveness 41
  - Discussion Questions 50
- Confess and Forsake – What is the Bible Teaching? 51
  - Confess and forsake 56
  - The Conviction of the Holy Spirit 61
  - Discussion Questions 66
- No more sacrifice for Sin 68
  - Understanding the Willful Sin 72
  - The Willful Sin 78
  - Discussion Questions: 83
- Works – Stepping Beyond the Achievement Perspective 85
  - Discussion Questions: 96
- No More Consciousness of Sin 98
  - Sin Conscious or Christ Conscious? 105
  - Discussion Questions: 112
- The Life that Pleases God 114
  - Discussion Questions: 124
- Consequences of Sin 126
  - The Carnal Christian 129
    - Christian Bondage 130
    - Inheritance 138
    - Chastisement 146
  - Discussion Questions: 151
- The Wayward Christian 154
  - Discussion Questions: 165
- Escaping the Law 166
  - Discussion Questions: 175

Persecution of Grace	177
Discussion Questions	190
Grace – The Reception of Perfection	191
Discussion Questions	198
The Mind of Christ	199
The Communion of the Spirit	203
The Revelation of the Spirit	206
Discussion Questions:	210
Becoming Spiritually Minded	211
Fleshly Minded	211
Spiritually Minded	213
Discussion Questions:	219

Grace is a Verb

I'm going to give away the plot of this book in the first chapter. By spoiling the surprise, I believe it will create an expectation of God's amazing gift of grace.

The gospel is not about what you do that meets God's approval, but what God has done for you. The word 'gospel' means 'good news.' Most presentations of the gospel focus on our sin, but the true message of grace is God's love. And the best part is that our sin is not a barrier to God's love. When our focus is on something other than God's love expressed through grace, true repentance is lost.

To get a better understanding, let's look at grace through the testimonies of two people. Doug is struggling with an alcohol addiction. It really doesn't matter what the addiction is, the principle applies. Whether Doug is on drugs, alcohol, or has a sexual addiction, or gambling addiction, the promise of God is, "Where sin abounds, grace even much more abounds."[1]

Doug became a Christian, and while the emotional joy of new found faith is running high, alcohol loses its appeal to him. Soon the emotions fade and Doug finds himself resisting the strong drawing of alcohol again. On a day of high stress, he gives in to one drink, and the next thing he knows, he's binge drinking again. Then he feels like a failure, and this causes him to seek even more relief through his addiction. But relief will never come through giving into his addiction.

At some point he will step out of the weakness of addiction and seek refuge through faith, but the rollercoaster Christianity has begun. Each time he falls, he feels rejected by God, and this makes him stand aloof from the Lord. He no longer feels accepted; therefore, he grows more and more distant from God, and wonders why he can't act like a Christian.

---

[1] Romans 5:20

At the other end of the defeatist scale is Susan. She has no outward signs of trouble. The church thinks of her as a gentle and kind person. People tell her how they wish they had her positive spiritual disposition, but instead of feeling encouraged, she feels like a hypocrite. At home she has trouble keeping her emotions in check. Stress builds up, and she quickly becomes angry toward her kids. She is snappy at her husband. The worst part is that she can't put her finger on a single cause of stress. She just starts feeling overwhelmed by life and can't help venting frustration toward those closest to her.

These types of situations play out in the lives of nearly every person – Christians included. Some addictions are clearly seen, such as substance abuse or destructive behaviors. However, some addictions are unnoticed by the church because they are acceptable. The workaholic is an addict. The one who needs constant affirmation is addicted to attention. The one who works in the church until they are burned out is fighting an addiction. Pride is approved as confidence. Neglecting the family in order to do church activity is considered spiritual. Judgmentalism is also a form of addiction. Every person has something in their life that overthrows their confidence in their relationship with God. Everyone has addictions of the flesh.

Here is the good news. Your weakness is not God's barrier. In fact, it is a tool in the hand of God that reveals the depth of His grace and love.

The problem is that the Dougs and Susans of the church have it backwards. They approach faith with the idea, "If I can only get this part of my life under control, I can be close to God."

This belief is in opposition to God's message of grace. God is not waiting for us to get our lives in order. In fact, God empowers these weaknesses of the flesh to become teachers who show you two important truths. One truth is that you and I are incapable of making ourselves acceptable to God. The second is, our weaknesses and failures prove the reality of God's unconditional love for us.

As long as you are trying to get your weaknesses under control, you are trying to live the Christian life by your own power. God then allows your sins, weaknesses, and failures to become tools to break your dependence off self so you are driven to look outside of your power and see the victory given to you by God's Spirit.

Until someone comes to the end of themselves, they tend to keep trying to force a spiritual standard upon their life in the flesh. It's a perpetual failing effort that does nothing more than create a rollercoaster faith. While the flesh is not seeking gratification, faith seems to succeed, but when the flesh arises, each person will discover that faith dependent upon self cannot keep the flesh in check.

The carnally focused person sees their sin and thinks, "God is angry at me." In reality God is using our sins to drive us to Christ, where love is exchanged for sin. Consider **Romans 7:12-14**

> [12] Therefore the Law *is* holy, and the commandment holy and just and good.
> [13] Has then what is good become death to me? Certainly not! But sin, that it might appear sin, was producing death in me through what is good, so that sin through the commandment might become exceedingly sinful.
> [14] For we know that the Law is spiritual, but I am carnal, sold under sin.

This is hard for people to understand, but the commandments of God, though good and holy, also serve to reveal to us how exceedingly sinful we are in the flesh. Yet we have it backwards. We think that when we see our failures, we are under God's condemnation, but the opposite is true. The purpose of our sins is to teach us how to trust fully in Christ. Look at **Galatians 3:24**

> Therefore the Law was our tutor *to bring us* to Christ, that we might be justified by faith.

The Law reveals our sin. Not only that, the commandments don't make us right with God, but instead they make us exceedingly sinful. They expose the truth that someone born in the flesh can never become spiritually righteous, thus revealing the depths of our sin and failure. When we see our shortcomings, sins, addictions, acts of ungodliness, and times we have completely blown it in our spiritual life, it is actually our tutor that reveals the love given to us through Christ.

When a person comes to the realization that they cannot make themselves righteous, it is then that they look to Christ and see grace. At the end of ourselves, when we think we are going to be swallowed up by failure, we find Christ. At the point of brokenness, Christ stands with the offer of grace – the great exchange. Christ gives us the offer of grace. Trade your sins, failures, shame, guilt, and your feeble attempts at righteousness, and give it to Him in exchange for perfect peace, complete faith, absolute righteousness, and every good thing of life. Let's add another passage that ties all of this together. Look at **2 Corinthians 12:9**

> And He said to me, "My grace is sufficient for you, for My strength is made perfect in weakness." Therefore most gladly I will rather boast in my infirmities, that the power of Christ may rest upon me.

This is the power of grace. When you fail, it isn't a defeat, but an opportunity to boast in your infirmities because they force you to trust in the power of Christ. Those who don't recognize their need also don't recognize the power of Christ that rests upon them. As long as you are living out the Christian life by your own power, your power is all you have. But when you see your utter incapacity to live by an eternal standard, then you also have eyes to see the power of God given to you.

People miss the power of God for one of two reasons. They either look to their own abilities and try to live out the Christian life by human effort, or they focus on their failures and erect sin as a barrier between themselves and God. In both cases, self is the focus, and we are the barrier. The barrier is not coming from God's side. And God will allow sin to linger in your life as long as you think you must accomplish holiness by your own efforts, for sin reveals the need for grace. And grace reveals the complete acceptance and deep love God has for us – apart from our abilities.

Failures should not defeat us. God knew our weaknesses before we knew Him. What's more, God promises that He will use our sins to teach us how to trust in Christ, and then when we trust Him, His power to defeat our flesh rests upon us. Grace works in our lives to defeat sin. I will reiterate this truth often – grace is the completed work of Christ, given to us as a free gift. Grace cannot be earned. It can only be received by faith. Grace cannot produce sin, for it is our escape from sin and the power of God within us that overcomes sin. This should be the natural result of becoming a child of God.

The reason Christians struggle and lack joy is because they don't understand the reality of God's completed work that has already been given to them. Many live like paupers in the Spirit because they can't see that they are children of promise.

We all hear that we are children of the King, but if this was truly believed, people would live in its reality. While we are grappling for acceptance, God has already granted it. We seek our own holiness, but we have been credited with God's own holiness. Most Christians strive to become righteous because they don't know how to receive God's righteousness.

In the New Testament we are told that we become the righteousness of God in Christ,[2] but this isn't merely a New Testament teaching. The Old Testament teaches that people are robed with God's righteousness.[3] What was promised in the Old Testament is now a reality in Christ. Look at this amazing promise of **Isaiah 54:17**

> No weapon formed against you shall prosper, And every tongue *which* rises against you in judgment You shall condemn. This *is* the heritage of the servants of the LORD, And their righteousness *is* from Me," Says the LORD.

This promise is packed full of truth. While it was spoken directly to the nation of Israel, God makes it clear that this is for all the servants of God. We serve God as children of promise, and one of the greatest promises we now have is that our

---

[2] 2 Corinthians 5:21
[3] Isaiah 61:10

righteousness is from God. Stop and meditate on that truth. It's not what you do. It's not based on who you are. It's not based on what you haven't done. Your righteousness is from God.

Not only do we have the promise of God's righteousness, but also the promise that the one who points at our failure to judge us will be defeated. Who raises his weapons against the Christian? Who is the one with the condemning tongue? Let's let the Bible answer this question. **Revelation 12:10**

> Then I heard a loud voice saying in heaven, "Now salvation, and strength, and the kingdom of our God, and the power of His Christ have come, for the accuser of our brethren, who accused them before our God day and night, has been cast down.

Satan is our accuser, but his testimony means nothing. He can only assault your emotions, but he cannot condemn you before God. Christ has already born your judgment and taken all sin out of the way.[4] This is why you have complete acceptance. You are the righteousness of God and what is of God is always fully accepted by God. What's more is that no weapon can overthrow God's declaration of your righteousness.

Our enemy accuses us night and day before God. According to Revelation 12:11, we overcome by Christ's blood and our testimony of faith in Him. If you are losing the battle against your flesh, emotions, or life in general, it is for one reason. You don't understand what you have been given. Look at the words of **2 Corinthians 10:3-4**

> [3] For though we walk in the flesh, we do not war according to the flesh.
> [4] For the weapons of our warfare *are* not carnal but mighty in God for pulling down strongholds,

Are you fighting in the flesh? Your efforts cannot win the war, for you will then be using the weakness of flesh to fight against the curse of sin. And the flesh is still under that curse. But you have a greater weapon – faith. Consider **1 John 5:4**

> For whatever is born of God overcomes the world. And this is the victory that has overcome the world-- our faith.

---

[4] Colossians 2:14

We'll visit these things in greater detail in later chapters, but take these truths to heart now. You are already an overcomer because your weapon is faith in the completed work of Christ. As you put your trust in what God has done, then you will begin walking in that victory. Then overcoming is the normal Christian life and not the distant hope that seems always out of reach.

Grace is an active verb because grace is action. It is God's action on your behalf. Jesus is the embodiment of grace, and He accomplished all things, fulfilled the Law, and we are made partakers of all He has provided.[5]

The grace of God is the gift of God's completed work, given to you, so you can now be a partaker of all God is bringing to fruition in this life and for the life to come. When a person learns to trust in God's work, by faith they receive that grace into their life. God's active grace not only transforms us into His likeness, but also becomes the accomplishing force in our lives to fulfill our role in God's will.

My prayer is that you will trust fully in Him and fulfill the life God has invited you to be a part of. The Christian life is not about what you can do for God. The Christian life is about receiving what God has done for you. God is glorified when you believe in His works, trust in them, and begin walking in Him. Confidence in Christ's completed work is the Christian walk.

Once you buy into the false notion that you must complete God's work, you have stepped outside of faith and are now trying to war according to the flesh. Even those who believe they are succeeding in religious efforts are working for this life only. True spirit-filled living is walking in faith. Disbelieving in Christ's work causes us to believe we must do something for God. Faith calls us to rest in complete confidence in Him. Then works becomes the grace of God working in us, instead of us presenting our human efforts to God.

If you have been raised in church, this might be a strange concept to grasp. The idea that we can't do anything for God may

---

[5] Hebrews 4:3, Hebrews 12:10, 2 Peter 1:4

raise questions, like what are we supposed to do? Does God's grace mean we just sit idly and wait for heaven?

These are questions I hope to answer in this book. The words of the Apostle Paul say it well in **1 Corinthians 15:10**
> But by the grace of God I am what I am, and His grace toward me was not in vain; but I labored more abundantly than they all, yet not I, but the grace of God *which was* with me.

The grace of God did something in Paul's life. The more Paul understood grace, the more it worked within him to produce good works. Before discovering grace, he labored for religion. He thought he was serving God, but he later said, "I count it all as trash." All his accomplishments were worthless because efforts of the flesh, even religious flesh, cannot accomplish the work of God.

Something about walking in grace drove him to labor more abundantly than all the others around him. And it's no coincidence that Paul explains grace in clearer terms than anyone else. Grace is active. It is active to reach us and rescue us from condemnation. Then it becomes active in our lives to fulfill our calling in God's plan. The only thing that prevents this from happening is to be distracted by the flesh.

Some are distracted by sin and they turn their backs on grace, thus hindering its transforming power in their lives. Some turn from grace because they begin trusting in religion and their own attempts to earn God's favor, also hindering the work of grace in their life.

The answer to both misconceptions is the same. Learn how to grow in grace and allow God's perfect work to complete us. Faith produces patience, and patience stills us from our own ways so God's work may complete its perfection in us.[6]

Grace is always an active verb, for it is the love of God, expressed through Christ and given to us in order to complete our transformation into His perfect image.

That's the 'fly over' view of this book. Now let's begin digging a little deeper so we can grow in grace!

---

[6] James 1:3-4

Discussion Questions:

Describe grace in your own words.

In what way is grace the expression of God's love?

What's the difference between believing in grace and receiving grace?

Think about any sin you may struggle with. Does this exclude you from fellowship with God? Or does it teach you that righteousness cannot come from your own abilities?

Is Christianity about accomplishing God's work, or receiving God's work? Explain your answer.

Does grace produce apathy?

Why do some claim to believe in grace, but it has no impact on their lives?

What does it mean to receive grace by faith?

Grasping Grace

Within your grasp, you already have the victory that overcomes the world. Failure in the Christian life is not a lack of churching, not the lack of righteousness, not the lack of opportunities, not the baggage of your past, and not the weaknesses that always seem to entangle you. In fact, failure itself is not your problem. It's the absence of trust that creates the vacuum that causes failure.

Darkness never fills a room. Light fills the room. Darkness is the absence of light. In the same way, failure is the absence of what creates success. Sin is the absence of righteousness. Doubt is the absence of faith. None of these things, darkness, failure, sin, or doubt have the power to overcome their counterparts. They only exist in the absence of the good God has provided.

Many Christians have wasted years, and sometimes an entire life, trying to overcome sin, fear, doubt, and other weaknesses of the flesh. The more you try to drive sin out of your life, the more sin will have victory.

Try this experiment, walk into a dark room and try to force darkness out. Speak rebuking words to it. Grab a broom and try to sweep it out. Try declaring the following, "Darkness, I refuse to accept you. You don't exist." It would be silly to do any of this. Yet this is exactly how most people approach the Christian life.

"Satan, I rebuke you," I've heard many Christian's say. Why? According to scripture, Jesus defeated Satan and all spiritual powers of wickedness on the cross.[7] We try to defeat a defeated foe. We try to muster up faith when faith has already been given. We try to become righteous even though the Bible says that we are the righteousness of God in Christ.[8] Satan can only step into a life that has stepped outside of Christ. He can lure, but he cannot overcome. Temptation is nothing more than casting bait in our

---

[7] Colossians 2:15
[8] 2 Corinthians 5:21

sight in the hopes that we'll turn from Christ and follow the bait. Satan flees God's presence, not our rebuking words.

Stop beating the air to chase away darkness, and just turn on the light switch. For the Christian, the light switch is faith. Faith is believing what God has declared and putting our trust in what He has done. Everything God accomplished through the life of Christ and the cross fulfills everything that pertains to the Christian life. And this is God's gift to you. Grace is God's favor, and that favor is expressed by the gifts of God's love invested in your life. You already have everything in Christ, but you must learn to trust in His grace – the unearned gift of His favor and works.

The revelation of grace is the most powerful truth in the Christian's life. People give a passing acknowledgment of grace, but few truly grasp the reality of it. Grace is normally defined as God's unmerited favor - which is true. However, very few Christians actually understand what this means in the normal Christian life. I say normal because these things apply to everyone and not just to the spiritually elite. It's a normal part of God's gift to His children, but it's a rare Christian indeed who truly comprehends the depth of this truth.

The average Christian looks at grace as God's gift of salvation through the cross. While this is part of grace, there is much more to discover. Grace is the completed work of Christ offered to us as the fulfillment of all that God desires for us to do and to be. It isn't just salvation, but the entirety of life. Everything Jesus accomplished was for us and is a gift of grace. This means that we have no need to accomplish anything in our lives to please God. It means we have been given all things that pertain to life and godliness. Take to heart the words of **2 Peter 1:3-4**

> [3] His divine power has given to us all things that *pertain* to life and godliness, through the knowledge of Him who called us by glory and virtue,
> [4] by which have been given to us exceedingly great and precious promises, that through these you may be partakers of the divine nature, having escaped the corruption *that is* in the world through lust.

How do you define all things? Is the promise most things? Many things? No. The Bible declares that we have been given all things that pertain to life *and* godliness. What does this exclude? Nothing. Everything you need to please God, to become an overcomer, live out the Christian life, and become spiritually mature has already been given to you.

You do not become more spiritual by doing more, but by learning how to become a partaker of God's own nature. It is by partaking of His divine nature that we escape corruption, live in the glory of God, have His virtue (or moral excellence) flowing through us, and receive all of God's promises. These are already yours. They are already mine. We miss the promises when we look to anything other than Christ. Only in Him do we have these things. Human effort and religion cannot provide success in the Christian life.

If we continue reading in 2 Peter, an interesting process of growth unfolds. Add to your faith virtue. Add to your virtue knowledge. Add to your knowledge self-control. On and on the process grows, but most of us miss the message being given in this passage. For many years I also missed the plainly stated truth because I looked at this as something I must do rather than what I must receive.

I looked at these things as a list of accomplishments, as though I must produce faith by personal effort. Then I must achieve moral excellence and add it to my faith. Then I must learn self-control and add it to my other accomplishments. This is an erroneous way of thinking.

Look at the foundation this passage is built upon. It begins with the foundational truth that Christ has given me all things. Then I am told that I receive by partaking of God's divine nature. Then I am told to add to my faith, virtue, and to virtual knowledge, and so on. Add, not achieve. Receive, not accomplish. That's the message.

When I have to do something for God, I am declaring that the work of Christ is not sufficient. When I fully understand grace, I understand the completed work of Christ and the glory of what

He has given to me. It is His virtue that is given to my faith. Don't forget that faith is also given to us by God (See Romans 12:3). God empowers us to believe by giving us eyes of faith. When we receive faith, we then have the power to begin receiving the grace of God.

This book will attempt to accomplish two main objectives. It will seek to teach you how to learn to trust in the grace of God given to you through Christ, and it will answer many misconceptions and objections brought up by legalistic religion regarding living by grace. It will answer the question, "If God has done all things, does this mean I become an apathetic Christian?" And the question, "How do God's commands apply to a true walk of grace?"

Many scriptures, interpreted through the lens of Western culture and man-centered works, can be confusing – unless we first understand the foundation of grace. We'll explore several passages that are misused and misunderstood, such as Hebrews 10 where people are taught that salvation is in jeopardy each time we sin. There are several passages that are misunderstood as being opposed to grace, and it's important that we understand these things so we can walk according to knowledge in faith and not according to legalism, which is dependent upon human effort.

A common objection to teaching grace is the belief that grace causes people to sin. It is said that if grace is taught the way the Bible appears to present it, grace will be misused as a license to sin. Nothing could be further from the truth. Grace is the power to overcome sin. Fully understanding grace strips away our desire to sin because it teaches us how to walk in the Spirit. Faith in God's grace is the reception of God's works.

Do we say that just believing in Christ for salvation teaches people to reject godliness? No. It's how we receive godliness. In the same way, putting our trust in Christ's work for the Christian life does not reject godliness, but empowers godliness in our lives.

Let's illustrate this with a word picture. What happens when people view something magnificent? They are naturally drawn into feelings of worship to some degree. When people see pictures of the Grand Canyon or Niagara Falls, it's a pretty picture. But when they stand at the cliffs of the canyon and see the enormity of it all, they are awestruck. They look hundreds of feet down and across miles of majestic canyons and then realize how the pictures did little to convey the inspiration of experiencing it in person. Pictures and descriptions can never capture the glory of direct experience.

When people see Niagara Falls in person, the magnificence becomes breath-taking. The roar of millions of gallons of water per minute pouring over 170 foot cliffs captivates the observer like no picture or video ever could.

Seeing pictures of mountains are lovely, but standing among the majestic peaks touches people deeply. Hearing about it, reading about it, seeing pictures of it cannot compare to actually experiencing it.

When people see the magnitude of these natural wonders, they are inspired and some people are changed. In the Psalms, David beheld the wonders of creation and said, "When I behold the works of your hands, the heavens, stars, moon, and all the works of your hands, what is man that you are mindful of him?" He was driven to worship by seeing the wonders of creation. Many have had similar experiences.

This also is the wonder of grace. Grace is the marvelous works of God, accomplishing everything we need, want, and even what we cannot yet imagine, and it is fully completed and presented to us as an unearned gift. Some only see in pictures. It sounds good, looks pretty, is somewhat inspiring, but it doesn't deeply touch their lives. They are not touched because they have only seen small glimpses through what others have presented, but have never seen it for themselves. Even if we see the works of Christ on the pages of scripture, if we are looking through the lens of legalism, we are peeking at the shadow of the promise and not beholding the real thing.[9]

People get small glimpses of grace, and in their minds, it is small. They know it's bigger than what they have seen through

---

[9] Hebrews 10:1

the pictures, but it's still theoretical and non-impacting. These are the ones who say that grace is not enough. They think that grace is a tool that helps us accomplish our own works because they have never seen the majestic works of God. For if someone even gets a glimpse of the works of God, they immediately realize how small and insignificant their own works and religious acts are.

Like David, when they see the magnitude of God's works, they look at their own feeble efforts and ask, what am I, and what is my work that God would be mindful of it? Yet that is the beauty of grace. While God's majesty reveals the insignificance of us and everything else in life, God's love has been revealed through grace – and grace says that God so loved us, that He gave all to reach us and bring us into His majesty. Then His call is to leave your feeble efforts behind and experience the wonders of His works. It is the receiving of grace that reveals our significance in God's plan.

Grace causes us to stand on the cliffs of spiritual life and marvel at what God has accomplished. Grace causes us to stand at the base of the raging flow of God's love expressed toward us and stand in awe. It causes us to gaze into the heavens of spiritual life and say, "When I see what God has already done, what can I do that is significant?" The answer is, nothing. Nothing except trust in His glory and receive the significance of His deep love.

God is not asking you to do anything for Him. God is inviting you to enter into His works and experience the incomprehensible depth of what He has done. It is for you. It is for me. God wants you to believe in His works and enter into it by faith. Consider this wonderful passage in **Hebrews 11:6**

> But without faith *it is* impossible to please *Him*, for he who comes to God must believe that He is, and *that* He is a rewarder of those who diligently seek Him.

How is God pleased? By what you do? By how much work you do for Him? No. God is pleased by faith. Faith is placing our confidence in God. It is to believe in His works deeply enough so that we put our confidence in what He has done. It is not to believe in our works and present them to God. Faith is the realization that grace has revealed the awe-inspiring works of God, and then resting in what He has done.

Grace is life-changing, for no one can view the works of God and desire the worthlessness of sin. Grace draws us into the works of God, and by default, we must step out of the works of sin. Rather than becoming a license to sin, grace displaces sin, for when we are awestruck by the magnitude of what God has already done, nothing else has much value.

And this is the heart of what I hope this book accomplishes. While I want to equip the reader with answers to questions about difficult scriptures, I especially want you to see and desire the works of God. Grace is the invitation of God to enter into His amazing works. Faith is how we enter into those works. When we see, we are given the power to believe, and then when we walk by faith, we please God. God is pleased when you join Him in the journey of love offered through the fellowship of Christ.

Yet grace, like faith, is something you cannot see until you step into it. God calls, invites, empowers us to receive, and then allows us to receive His call, or choose another way. Many voices beckon to us, but the only true calling comes through the cross. Those who believe God will have their eyes opened. Consider **Luke 19:26**

> For I say to you, that to everyone who has will be given; and from him who does not have, even what he has will be taken away from him.

In Christ, we have received what has been given by God. Outside of Christ, even that which seems to have value will one day come to nothing. As you believe, you step into the world of faith. God reveals His works and will to you, and then calls you to receive it. The world calls with many distractions. Religion – even that which claims the name of Christ – is one of those distractions. God says to trust in Him, but religion calls for us to accomplish through our efforts.

Those who choose religion often seem to have received, but when the fruit of their labors come to maturity, they will recognize that what they thought they had was nothing but ashes of human effort. Because they did not have what God provided, what they thought they had will come to nothing.

Those who have faith will follow God's call. Not only will they experience what God called them to find, but they quickly see how that invitation was only the introduction to what God is giving them. Then those who have what was received by faith will be given even more.

God wants you to receive His works and benefits. These are not things God merely gives to those who earn them. God doesn't look upon those who receive of Him as selfish. No. Those who have faith in His works, have faith in Him. It is not possible to receive what God offers without receiving through the relationship of God's fellowship.

When you receive of God, you are also receiving God's relationship that has been given to you. Then entering into His works is not merely a quest for a benefit, but it is an act of worship. The receiver of God's divine nature is drawn into a heart of worship and can do nothing other than stand in amazement of who God is and what He has done. Without this understanding, we are left skimming the surface of Christianity and never discover the value of God's love.

Grace is not a selfish gospel, but an invitation into a lifestyle of worship. In grace, there is no sin, no condemnation, and no limitations. Grace draws us right into the depths of our God-given relationship so we can be the child of the inheritance, which God designed all of creation to provide to His children.

Grace is the only doctrine that truly gives God the glory for all He has done. Everything else robs God's glory and replaces it with man's achievement. The work of man is the main focus of false Christianity. True Christianity is focused on the work of Christ. Grace is God's work, given to you, so you can experience all that He is. He made you into a child of the Kingdom so He can enjoy fellowship with you. Until you understand grace, you will never fully experience the Kingdom of God. Let's conclude this chapter with **Luke 17:20-21**

> [20] Now when He was asked by the Pharisees when the kingdom of God would come, He answered them and said, "The kingdom of God

> does not come with observation;
> [21] "nor will they say, `See here!' or `See there!' For indeed, the kingdom of God is within you."

The Bible *does* teach that one day the Kingdom of God will be seen with our eyes, but we don't have to wait for eternity to begin experiencing God's Kingdom. Once you are a child of God in Christ, the Kingdom is already reality within you through God's Holy Spirit. The invitation of grace is to begin experiencing what you already have based on who you already are.

May God reveal the reality of this walk of faith as you prayerfully explore the principles explained in this book.

Discussion Questions

If light dispels darkness, and the gospel is called the light, what happens to sin when someone walks in the light of the gospel?

Must we deal with sin in order to receive grace?

If we are partakers of God's nature, what can we do that makes our lives more godly?

If God has given us all things that pertain to life and godliness, what does this leave for us to provide?

If I must do something for God, is Christ's work complete?

Does grace produce apathy? Why or why not?

Some people claim to be grace-believing Christians, but show no evidence of Christ-likeness. Why do you think this happens?

How are we in the Kingdom now? How can we live in a fallen world and still experience the Kingdom of God?

Assurance of Grace

Grace *is* the foundation of the Christian life. In fact, grace *is* the Christian life. Because of many misconceptions of grace that lead to objections by well meaning Christians, I see the need for more clarification. We'll explore this life-changing truth so more people can have the joy of deep fellowship with God without legalism and fear, while also learning how to keep human effort from interfering with the work of God in their lives.

When grace is not understood, people assume it is a license to sin, or that grace is God giving Christians the ability to keep the Law – not understanding that Christ has already fulfilled all of the Law on our behalf. Jesus said, "You shall know the truth, and the truth shall set you free." Understanding this vital truth frees you from both sin and legalism, from religion and non-religion, and from both sin and self-righteousness.

It's the truth that sets you free – not figuring out what the lie is. Many lose sight of the truth because they become distracted by the quest to expose lies. It's far too easy to spend so much time looking for errors in others that some have the joy of truth crowded out of their life. I know this from personal experience. Yet when a person grasps the truth of grace, nothing in their life will be the same. And once truth flourishes, false beliefs are dethroned and displaced from the heart of the believer.

Grace teaches you to stop running from God and come confidently to Him. Grace shines the light on scripture and opens our understanding. Consider the often recited passage of **Hebrews 4:16**

> Let us therefore come boldly to the throne of grace, that we may obtain mercy and find grace to help in time of need.

Most Christians quote this passage thinking it applies to meeting our earthly needs, but this is not what this passage is focusing upon. The throne of grace is for *mercy* during our time of need. Indeed we do go to the Lord for all our needs – physical and spiritual, but don't miss the beauty of this truth.

When people know they have fallen short of God's standard, they often feel shame, guilt, or failure. Or sometimes all three. Instead of approaching God with confidence, they don't feel worthy. Let's take a moment to focus on two words from this passage that especially apply to our daily lives. Boldly and grace. The word 'boldly' comes from the Greek word 'parrēsia', which means just what it says: confidence, assurance, and boldness. It does not mean timidity, fear, or arrogance.

The word for grace is the Greek word 'charis' which means: graciousness, acceptance, benefit, and favor. It does not mean greed, selfishness, or merit.

The message is that we should have confidence to come before the throne of grace knowing we are welcomed and have the assurance that God will not only receive us, but that He wants us there. It's an act of faith to come confidently before God when we have need of mercy. Mercy is to be spared the penalty for what we should receive, and grace is to be given the benefits of God that we do not deserve. Both are part of the Christian life and both are received through confident faith in this promise.

Don't lose sight of the phrase, "obtain mercy and find grace to help in the time of need." Even when we fall short and blow it badly, we still should have the faith to come before God with confidence. It's fine to sorrow over our sin, but it's not okay to take off God's robe of righteousness and declare the work of Christ as nullified in our lives.

When God revealed His work to Peter in the book of Acts, God declared, "What God has cleansed, you must not call common." To call something common is to declare it unclean or unholy. Once God has cleansed a person (even ourselves), to declare that work as common is to show despite to the Spirit of grace. We'll dig deeply into this later.

To refuse to come confidently before the throne of grace in our time of need is a rejection of faith. The throne of God is not for those who have achieved a higher spirituality. It's for anyone who is in Christ. Whether you are a new Christian, a mature Christian, or a fallen Christian, if you have been born into the

Spirit, you MUST believe God's word and count the throne of grace as a place of fellowship. When you blow it, you need grace. When you are doing well, you still need grace.

The Christian life is not about what you have done or can do for God. The Christian life is about what Jesus has done for you. Grace is the work of Christ given to you and brought to maturity in you. Grace is the completed work of God given to your account as a gift of His love.

Let's contemplate the depth of grace for a moment. We looked at the translation of the word 'grace', but in simplest terms, it means the unmerited (or unearned) favor of God. What most Christians don't understand is how deep that favor goes. Grace is a person, and his name is Jesus. Jesus is the gift of God to the world. He is the embodiment of the work and righteousness of God, and any who are in Christ have ceased from their labors because they have entered into His completed life and work.[10]

To fully define grace, we must understand that grace is the completed work of Jesus Christ that has been given to you. Holiness is the gift of God given to you through Christ. Righteousness is the gift of God, given to you through Christ. Sanctification is the gift of God, given to you through Christ. Faith is a gift of God. Everything acceptable to God has been accomplished through Christ and given to you without your merits.

This is the work of God – that you believe on Jesus Christ (John 6:28-29). Most of the religious leaders of Jesus' day never found righteousness because they pursued their own righteousness instead of the righteousness given by God.[11] When Jesus taught in the temple, He warned the people, "Unless your righteousness exceeds the righteousness of the Pharisees, you cannot enter into the Kingdom of Heaven."[12]

Because we always hear about the Pharisees in a negative light, we don't understand the magnitude of this statement. There

---

[10] Hebrews 4:10
[11] Romans 10:3
[12] Matthew 5:20

were hundreds of Pharisees and many were sincerely trying to serve God. We notice the ones who stood up as enemies against Jesus, but Nicodemus came to Jesus in his quest to find truth. Joseph the Pharisee became a disciple of Christ and took part in Jesus' burial, even providing his own family tomb to Jesus after the crucifixion.

The Apostle Paul was a Pharisee before coming to Christ. Based on his own testimony, he was driven to serve God by stamping out the Christian sect because it was a threat to the religious system God had established in the Old Testament. While he was a Pharisee, he didn't understand that the Law served to bring us to Christ.

It was Paul who said of the Pharisees, "Because they are seeking to establish their own righteousness, they did not find the righteousness of God." And the same is true for anyone who seeks to establish their own righteousness in our day.

When Jesus declared that our righteousness must exceed that of the Pharisees, the people were amazed. These were men who dedicated their lives to studying the scriptures. Their goal was to make sure the Law God established in the Old Testament was obeyed to the letter. They knew the text of the Old Testament by memory. Their entire lives centered around religion and serving in the temple and synagogues. What could anyone do that these men weren't already doing? If our righteousness must exceed the righteousness of those who were the pinnacle of religious thought, who can be saved? What more could anyone listening to Jesus do that these men weren't already doing?

And that is the point. The answer is 'nothing'. There is nothing those listening to Jesus could do to exceed the religious efforts of the Pharisees. If dedication to religion can't make us right with God, what can?

The point is that human effort cannot accomplish the work of God. And this was the point that Paul, the ex-Pharisee was making. Because they were working to establish their own righteousness, they missed true righteousness – that which is a gift of God.

You are the same. If you try to merit God's favor in any way, you are denying the work of Christ. The more you try to establish your own righteousness, the more you will miss the righteousness of God. And that is the message of grace. The Law system served many purposes, but this is the main purpose – to show us our need of Christ.

According to the Bible, if you break the Law on any point, you aren't just guilty of that point – you are guilty of breaking the whole law. This is why legalism is an absurd human effort.

To illustrate this, let's consider the Sabbath. Sabbath keeping is a growing trend in modern Christianity, so it is a good example of the church's attempt to mix law into Christianity. Some argue that in order to keep ourselves in God's favor, we must keep the Sabbath, but Sabbath observers are not keeping the Sabbath. Do they prepare food? Do they drive cars? Do they buy or sell anything? According to the Law God gave of the Sabbath, each person must abide in their home and do nothing. No playing games, no setting the table, no clean up, no going to the store, no traveling more than a short walk to church, no nothing. Even to buy any product or service on the Sabbath is a violation of this law.[13] And if you do anything – even one time – you have broken the Sabbath and are a law-breaker.

But Jesus said that He is not only the Lord of the Sabbath, but He is that rest. That is what the word 'Sabbath' means – rest. We keep the Sabbath by entering into Christ where we rest from our labors of human effort and receive the gift of Christ's completed work.

The Bible says that those who are in the Spirit are no longer under the Law.[14] Those who are in the flesh are under the Law, but those who have died to the flesh have been set free from the Law.[15] Once we enter Christ, we have kept the Law, for we have entered into His works and ceased from our own. Jesus is the Sabbath rest, and any who are in Christ by faith have kept the

---

[13] Nehemiah 10:31
[14] Galatians 5:18, Romans 8:4
[15] Romans 7:5-6

whole law – including the Law of the Sabbath. Any who attempt to keep the Sabbath by human effort have not trusted in Christ and are denying His works. According to Romans 10:4, "Christ is the end of the Law to everyone who believes."

The Law was never intended to make people righteous. The Law is intended to show people that they are not righteous. You don't earn rewards for keeping the Law, you can only be penalized. And this is why most people have the wrong perspective. Many believe God uses the Law to reward them for doing good, but the Law has no merits. The Law takes people out of righteousness when it's broken. It never makes a sinful person righteous. The Law only exposes the flaws of human nature. Look at **Romans 3:19**

> Now we know that whatever the Law says, it says to those who are under the Law, that every mouth may be stopped, and all the world may become guilty before God.

The Law doesn't make us righteous, it exposes our inability to keep the Law, and because we fail to keep it, we are declared guilty. And every mouth is stopped so that no one can say, "I have made myself righteous." We are guilty before we even understand what we should keep. Even if we were innocent when we found the Law, who could stand? Who cannot sin? Who doesn't act or think selfishly?

Let's go back to the idea of Sabbath keeping Christians. The religions that focus on the Sabbath only focus on the things they can keep, but no one has the right to alter the Law to fit their lifestyle or conform it to modern culture. Christian Sabbath observers still drive to church. They still hand out bulletins. They still work to get themselves and their kids dressed and ready.

The Law doesn't merely say to perform worship services on the Sabbath. The Law says that we must do no work on the Sabbath. The Law says that you cannot work, nor can your children do any work, nor strangers with you, nor your livestock. As previously mentioned, even making a purchase is a violation of the Sabbath. What if your kids are sick and you need medicine or a doctor visit? There are no exceptions. What if you are about to run out of gas? No exceptions. Did you know it is even a violation to pick up sticks on the Sabbath? See Numbers 15:32-35. Not one Sabbath only church fully keeps the Sabbath as it is dictated in the Law.

I'm driving this point home because you must see the purpose of the Law, for you do not want to be under that system. Without an infallible nature the Law is not your ally.

So why did God choose to drive us to grace instead of making a merit system? While we can't know all of God's reasons for how He established creation, we can know what He has revealed. Ultimately, we were created to experience the fullness of God. That fullness can't be realized until we see the amazing truth of grace. Grace can't be understood until we recognize that everything outside of God is insufficient. Freedom is always more valuable to those who have escaped oppression.

The message of the Law is that you can never be righteous because you fall short of God's glory. Works by human effort creates self-righteousness, but the Law dismantles it. The message of the Law is that you are not good enough and you can never be good enough. It exposes the vast gap between flawed human nature and God's perfect nature. The Law serves to expose your sin and the weakness of human nature.

The message of grace is that God has done it all. He created all things and did so for His pleasure. Part of all things includes the work of God which He established in creation. Not only should we stand upon majestic mountains and marvel at the beauty of the physical world, but we also should stand upon the mountain of grace and marvel at the wonders of what God has done for us.

When you behold the holiness of your life in Christ, you will stand in awe of the work of God, which He has done for you to enjoy. When you behold the righteousness of Christ given to you, you'll stand amazed at the work of God established for you to enjoy. Every godly thing that is part of the Christian life is the work of God, accomplished on your behalf so you can gaze over the spiritual side of creation and soak in the beauty of God's works.

Most Christians never experience the beauty of grace because they are so busy trying to establish their own works that they miss the works of God. You are the Pharisee when you are self-focused. I am a Pharisee when I am looking at my sins and failures, or my works and righteousness. While I'm looking at me, I cannot see or experience the works of God.

Again I say that this is the message of grace. It is to learn how to behold the glory of God and rest in His goodness. Grace is the work of Christ, done for you, so you can have fellowship with God and experience His fullness in your life. When you understand grace, everything that is not of God falls away. All that is of God will begin to emerge. Grace teaches you how to rest from your labors and trust in God's. Grace defeats sin and establishes you in His righteousness. Judgmentalism dies and a love for the brethren emerges. Grace *is* the Christian life. Anything else robs you of God's glory.

Grace is the only truth that gives God all the glory. And when God is glorified, we are partakers of that benefit. My prayer is that you develop a deeper understanding of God's work so that His grace can transform you and that you have fullness of joy – just as God has promised!

Discussion Questions

What is the purpose or purposes of the Law?

Can keeping the Law make a sinner righteous?

Can a violation of the law make a righteous person a sinner?

Why is the Law fulfilled in Christ?

What does it mean, "For Christ is the end of the law for righteousness to everyone who believes?" (See Romans 10:4)

Read Galatians 5:3 and James 2:10. Can someone pick only certain parts of the Law without placing themselves under the weight of the whole Old Testament legal system?

Transformation of Grace

Let's begin this chapter with a word-picture. I'm going to reuse an illustration from a previous book because it beautifully introduces the transforming power of grace. It's the tale of two husbands.

A woman married a husband who was very demanding. This man was perfect. He had an infallible nature and not only did he not make mistakes, but his nature prevents him from ever making a mistake. She discovered that her husband was actually a employed to enforce laws that judged anyone who could not mirror God's perfect nature. Unfortunately, she was born with a human nature and could not be perfect, thus making her incompatible with her husband.

Her husband had no tolerance for imperfection. He pointed out every flaw she had. He was perfect and could only accept perfection. Every flaw, failure, and mistake was brought to the light and exposed for her to see. The criticism of her husband did not make her better, it made her worse. The more she looked at his perfection, the more she saw her own failure. The more she failed, the more her husband condemned her. It was not a love relationship; it was a miserable existence.

One day another man came into her life. He loved her with such a love that he would sacrifice everything for her good. He saw her weaknesses, but wanted to lift her up instead of beating her down. She loved this man, but according to the law, she cannot divorce and remarry, for that is adultery. This man, being righteous, cannot enter into an adulterous relationship.

The law declares that she is bound to her husband as long as he lives. Only if her husband dies could she be married to another, but her husband is eternal. He cannot die, for he is the mirror of God's eternal nature.

The one she loves cannot marry her because she is bound to her husband. Her husband cannot love her because her nature is incompatible with his nature. He cannot die, so what can she do?

The man who loves her provided the perfect solution. The only solution. He would die for her. That would pay the penalty of the Law. And that is who her husband is – the Law. The Law demands judgment for every failure. She cannot be loved because the penalty must first be judged. Unfortunately, the wages of sin (breaking the Law) is death. But the man she loves has agreed to take that penalty upon himself, which will eliminate the judgment due to her, but it will not free her from her husband, the Law. Since her nature is imperfect, she will fail again, and the next mistake she makes will only create a new penalty and the cruel relationship will continue.

To solve this problem, her love, who is grace, points out an important part of the law. He who has died is free from the law. Her husband cannot die, but if she dies, she will be freed from the law that bound her to the cruel husband of the law. So Grace invites her to die with Him. He promises that if she dies with Him, He will raise her up with himself. He also is eternal and has the power to lay down His life and take it up again. Not only that, but because He is the possessor of life, He can raise her up into a new life, born in the likeness of God's nature where she can be compatible with her new husband.

She is crucified together with Him, buried with Him, her old life is now dead, and she is freed from the Law. She becomes a new life and is born into a new nature. This new life is not born under the Law, but born under grace. She then is joined to a new husband who loves her. Instead of criticizing her failures, He took her failures away and replaced it with a new life that draws from His eternal power.

And this is the conflict between the Law and Grace. The Bible says that we die to our old life when we are buried with Christ in baptism, and we are raised as a new creation. Our new life is based on His eternal power and we are partakers of His divine nature.

The Law cannot make anyone righteous; it only criticizes our human nature. Grace doesn't fix the old nature, it buries it and invites us into a new life where we can become a partaker of God's divine nature.[16]

This begs the question. If we have died in Christ and have been set free from the taskmaster of the Law, why would we want to submit back to that old husband? Keep in mind that the life of the flesh, which was married to the old husband, is dead. Our new life was never under the Law, so submitting to another husband is unfaithfulness to our marriage in Christ. Placing ourselves back under the Law is like having an affair against Christ.

Romans 6:14 clearly states that in Christ, we are no longer under the Law, but under grace. And the result is that sin can no longer have dominion over us. That is the product of the Law – it puts us under the curse of sin. Galatians 3:10 says that those who are under the works of the Law are under the curse. Romans 3:19 tells us that the Law speaks to those who are under the Law – which is not the Christian. Scripture also teaches that the Law cannot justify anyone, it can only bring about the knowledge of sin and then condemn violators – for all have sinned.[17]

Finally, Romans 5:20 tells us that the Law entered that sin might abound. Are you getting the picture? While many churches teach that you must keep the Law in order to be righteous, the Bible says that those who are under the Law are cursed. Then it is sin, not righteousness, that abounds.

It is often said that grace is abused and made into a license to sin, but the opposite is true. The Law causes the weakness of human nature to sin, but grace transforms us into Christ's likeness. The person under the Law says, "I can do it. I can make myself righteous," but God rejects all works under the Law. As stated earlier, the Law doesn't merit righteousness. The Law merely reveals law breaking and lawbreakers. The Law is just a litmus test. When it's applied, it says either "Yes, this person is perfect," or "No, I found a flaw. They are corrupt." And only one person passed the test of the Law. Christ fulfilled the Law because

---

[16] 2 Peter 1:4
[17] Romans 3:20

His nature was already perfect. The Law merely agreed that His nature was perfect. It did not make Him perfect.

New Creation

In order to understand the Christian life, we must understand that it is a new life – a new birth. This is explained in **2 Corinthians 5:16-17**

> [16] Therefore, from now on, we regard no one according to the flesh. Even though we have known Christ according to the flesh, yet now we know *Him thus* no longer.
> [17] Therefore, if anyone *is* in Christ, *he is* a new creation; old things have passed away; behold, all things have become new.

Just as Christ was glorified after His death and is no longer viewed through the eyes of flesh, we also are no longer viewed through eyes of flesh. This is of vital importance in regards to each other as well as how we view ourselves.

When someone comes to Christ, everything in their old life has passed away. We no longer view them as the person they were, but as the person they are in Christ. The new man is a new birth where nothing from the flesh can be carried forward. Not wrongs. Not works. No sin or action of the flesh passes into the new life of the Spirit.

You once had one nature – a sinful nature inherited through the flesh. Now you still have only one nature, but it is a new nature, born through Christ. This is explained in **Romans 6:5-7**

> [5] For if we have been united together in the likeness of His death, certainly we also shall be *in the likeness* of *His* resurrection,
> [6] knowing this, that our old man was crucified with *Him*, that the body of sin might be done away with, that we should no longer be slaves of sin.
> [7] For he who has died has been freed from sin.

Our old nature has been crucified and buried – not will be. If you are in Christ, this is already an accomplished fact. It is important to understand these things or else the Biblical principles we'll be discussing won't make sense.

The old man (our old nature) was put to death with Christ. Just as you died with Christ through His death, through His resurrection you also are now raised as a new creation. The body of sin has been done away with and you now live according to a new nature. This will be very significant when we view the Holy Spirit's work later in this book.

Since we still live in a body born under the corruption of sin, the deeds of the old man still arise and tempt us to view life through the flesh again. This is not the old nature, but as the Bible says in Romans 7:17-25, it is no longer you, but sin dwelling in your body, warring against your mind and trying to regain control. But as we renew our minds in Christ, that conduct is cast off and we live according to our new nature. Consider **Ephesians 4:22-24**

> [22] that you put off, concerning your former conduct, the old man which grows corrupt according to the deceitful lusts,
> [23] and be renewed in the spirit of your mind,
> [24] and that you put on the new man which was created according to God, in true righteousness and holiness.

Notice that this is the conduct associated with the old nature and not the nature itself. Our flesh carries the habits of the old nature, though the nature itself is dead. Throughout the New Testament, we are told to put off that old conduct and take on that which is born out of the new man. The new nature is born of God, is a partaker of God's nature, has its life from God, and is incorruptible. 1 Peter 1:23 tells us that we are born again from an incorruptible seed by the Holy Spirit. This is also explained in **1 John 3:9**

> Whoever has been born of God does not sin, for His seed remains in him; and he cannot sin, because he has been born of God.

The inner man cannot sin because it is born of God. Our new nature is in Christ by the Holy Spirit. It is eternal, incorruptible, and has perfect fellowship with God. Our new nature has to be incorruptible, otherwise we would be in the same condition as before. Sin is through the body, but holiness is through the Spirit. That which is joined to God is incorruptible and that which was corrupted was put to death in Christ.

The Bible says the wages of sin is death. Anyone outside of Christ is under the curse of death. Any who are in Christ have already died, for we were crucified with Christ. He suffered death, which is the wage (or payment) of sin. By faith we surrender sin to Him and inherit righteousness from Him. When we enter God's covenant of faith, God purges our old nature and places a new nature within us. That new nature has constant fellowship with the Holy Spirit. Even if we sin in the body, we cannot break that fellowship. There are consequences to sin, but these can never undo the work of Christ. Nor can sin transform the spirit we have received from God into a sinfully corrupted nature.

If you are in Christ, you are a new creation. The gospel message for you is to learn of Christ so you can walk as the new person who has been born of God according to an incorruptible nature. The greater part of that walk is enjoying the fellowship you have with God. Ignorance of that fellowship is the only reason Christians don't experience the deeper walk of the Spirit.

Did the Law come to an end?

Once, after explaining what has been discussed here, a man challenged the doctrine of grace saying, "Jesus said that heaven and earth will pass away, but the Law will never pass away. How can you claim that the Christian is no longer under the Law?" He went on to claim that this teaching on grace means the Law has come to an end, and he believed this to be false. He believed that the Christian is empowered to keep the Law, but was still obligated to the Law.

Let me be clear on this. The Law has not passed away. As stated earlier, the Law is eternal. The Law is just as powerful today as it was in the Old Testament times. The Law will never pass away. It is the old nature that passes away, and according to the Bible, "Those of us who are led by the Spirit are not under the Law."[18] It's the new nature, born under Christ, that enters the

---

[18] Galatians 5:18

new covenant of grace. Our old nature could never escape the Law, but our new nature is of God and not bound to the law, which was sent forth to condemn the flesh.

I say that the Law hasn't passed away, but for the Christian it has. In 2 Corinthians 3:7-18 the Bible teaches that the glorious law written in stone and given through Moses is passing away, but that which has now come through Christ remains and is more glorious than the passing Law. Jesus fulfilled the Law, and those who enter Christ have died to the Law and are now under a new law – the Law of faith.[19] The old Law stands against those who are in the flesh, but is fully satisfied through those who are in Christ by faith.

The problem is that the Law is spiritual and eternal. Those who are not in the Spirit can never keep the Law. Those who are in Christ have already fulfilled the Law, for we died to the flesh and are in Christ, who has already fulfilled the Law. Look at **Romans 7:14**

> For we know that the Law is spiritual, but I am carnal, sold under sin.

This is why the Law cannot justify a man. The person born under sin is contrary to the Law and even if we could keep the Law of God, our past sins would still stand up and condemn us. Yet even with the power of the Holy Spirit, there is not one person who has kept the Law, for we all are drawn back into sin from time to time. The purpose of the Law was to keep us restrained while being a teacher that explained our inability to measure up to God, and then pointed us to Christ. Look at **Galatians 3:23-25**

> [23] But before faith came, we were kept under guard by the Law, kept for the faith which would afterward be revealed.
> [24] Therefore the Law was our tutor *to bring us* to Christ, that we might be justified by faith.
> [25] But after faith has come, we are no longer under a tutor.

Notice that last sentence. After faith has come, we are no longer under the tutor. The Law was once the tutor of man, but faith in Christ takes us out of the Law and puts us in the Spirit.

---

[19] Romans 3:27

To those who believe that faith empowers them to uphold the Law, Galatians 4:21 asks an interesting question. You who desire to be under the Law, do you not hear the Law? There are two types of children, those under the Law and those under the promise. Those under the Law can never be free.

But don't take my word for it. Let's look at how the apostles dealt with this very question. As the gospel spread, many gentiles (or non-Jews) began coming to faith in Christ. Many Jewish Christians came into the gentile churches and taught them that they must not only believe in Christ, but that they must also keep the Law. Some of the early missionaries confronted this false teaching and it became a big controversy in the church.

Some believed faith was part of the Law – just as we see people saying today. Others said that Jesus was the fulfillment of the Law, believed in His completed work, and accurately believed that trusting in the Law was disbelief in Christ's fulfillment of the Law.

It became such an issue that all the apostles met together with all the church leaders and elders. They searched the scriptures and each person shared. The elders and the apostles, who were taught directly from Jesus, came to a consensus and settled on this message sent to the gentile Christians in **Acts 15:28-31**

> [28] For it seemed good to the Holy Spirit, and to us, to lay upon you no greater burden than these necessary things:
> [29] that you abstain from things offered to idols, from blood, from things strangled, and from sexual immorality. If you keep yourselves from these, you will do well. Farewell.
> [30] So when they were sent off, they came to Antioch; and when they had gathered the multitude together, they delivered the letter.
> [31] When they had read it, they rejoiced over its encouragement.

Do you notice anything absent from this letter to the gentile churches? Where is the Law? Where are the rules and regulations? "We lay on you no other burden." No Old Testament law. No list of rules. The only things they presented were the things that distracted people from Christ. Other than that, no other burden was needed.

Scripture does not teach us how to keep rules and regulations. It teaches us how to trust fully in Christ and His completed work. Everything else leads us away from the things that draw us outside of Christ and puts our focus back on the flesh and a dying world. You have been given all things pertaining to life and godliness.

The work is completed. Now it's time to learn how to walk in the Spirit through the gift of grace. Anything that distracts us from grace is an unnecessary burden. This includes both sin and religious efforts. Even the Law is a distraction from Christ if we turn back to it for salvation, to achieve righteousness, or to merit God's favor. The call of the gospel is to trust completely in Christ and allow Him to transform us into His likeness.

Discussion Questions

Is the Law of the Old Covenant intended to make people right with God, or to test each person to prove their perfection or imperfection?

If the Bible calls us a new creation, what happened to the old nature?

How did the Law tutor us so we could see and receive grace?

Read Romans 10:4. In what way has the law come to an end? Who does this apply to?

Why can't the non-Christian (those with the old nature) keep the law?

How does the Christian keep the law?

Read Romans 3:25-28. What law is the Christian under? Explain.

Understanding Complete Forgiveness

It's difficult to determine which should be explained first, how we deal with sin, or how we understand forgiveness. When forgiveness is taught the way the Bible explains it, people naturally have objections like, "What about sin? Does complete forgiveness mean that sin no longer matters? Does total forgiveness mean I can live any way I want?"

These are normal questions when discussing Christ's completed work of forgiveness. If you have been raised in church, you'll likely have objections as I present scriptures that undermine the common thought of sin and forgiveness. In the next chapter, the most common of these concerns will be addressed.

It's vital to first understand forgiveness, for it is the foundation we stand upon as we press ahead into maturity in Christ.

One thing I have learned is that when I didn't understand forgiveness, I never had confidence in my relationship with God. When I felt unworthy of God because of my failures, instead of turning to God for strength, I distanced myself from Him out of shame, fear, and guilt. My perception of God's disappointment in my performance hindered my ability to overcome sin. It did not make me less likely to sin.

What happens when a child has done something they are afraid will lead to punishment? Very young children hide. They don't want the parent to find them. Older children hide the evidence, hoping their parents won't find out. Sometimes they suffer needless consequences because a parent doesn't find out until the harm of consequences begins coming to light. Many times the child finds out the parent would have gladly helped them overcome, but out of fearful guilt, they suffered needlessly. When a child understands their parent's total acceptance, they will face their failure and seek help.

We have a High Priest who has lived among people and can identify with our sufferings.[20] Christ not only accepts us, warts and all, but He is our advocate, helper, and deliverer.

Unlike human parents, God not only can identify with our sufferings of life's temptations, but He is perfect in nature and does not lash out with anger or get frustrated. People get frustrated because their expectations are not met, or they can't regain control of situations.

God has no unrealistic expectations, for He already sees the end of all things, and has seen it from the beginning.[21] God cannot be frustrated, for His purposes are already established into creation. He cannot be disappointed in you, for He knew your actions before you made your mistakes. And He has already built into your path the way of escape and recovery into His perfect will.

And this is where we begin the quest to understand total forgiveness. It is an accomplished fact because God already knew your sins from before creation, and every sin was credited to Christ's account and then paid publicly on the cross at His death.

Keep this one thing in mind, every sin you have committed was paid for on the cross two-thousand years ago. Before you were born, Jesus had already atoned for your sin. Every one of your sins were in the future when Jesus paid the debt of sin. In fact, the Bible says that Jesus atoned for sin (singular) not sins (plural). Look at **Romans 8:3-4**

> [3] For what the Law could not do in that it was weak through the flesh, God *did* by sending His own Son in the likeness of sinful flesh, on account of sin: He condemned sin in the flesh,
> [4] that the righteous requirement of the Law might be fulfilled in us who do not walk according to the flesh but according to the Spirit.

Jesus did not die for your sins. He did not atone for your sins. It was sin as a whole – all rebellion against God – that was dealt with. I have heard this message preached many times, "When you sin, Jesus reapplies the blood when you confess your

---

[20] Hebrews 2:17, Hebrews 4:14
[21] Isaiah 46:9-10

sins and repent." I have also taught this type of doctrine before I understood the Bible's teaching.

This sounds good only because we have not truly looked at what the scriptures are teaching. God works in our individual lives to bring us into intimate fellowship with Himself, but when it comes to sin, it is not on an individual basis. Sin entered the world, and through sin, death reigned. According to the Bible, death reigned through one person – Adam – but that curse affected all of mankind. Look at **Romans 5:17**

> For if by the one man's offense death reigned through the one, much more those who receive abundance of grace and of the gift of righteousness will reign in life through the One, Jesus Christ.

Death reigned through one, but grace now reigns through one. In Adam all die, much more in Christ shall all be made alive. [22] Those who are in Adam are under sin. Those who are in Christ are under grace. There is no atoning for each individual sin. Sin – singular – is atoned for, and any who are in Christ have escaped Adam's sin and are now under the righteousness of Christ.

In John 8:34 Jesus said that those who commit sin are slaves of sin. In Romans 6, the Bible explains that we were under slavery to sin, and anyone who turns back to sin is submitting back under slavery. But any who submit to Christ are no longer under bondage to sin. Individual sins are acts of submission back into bondage, but we are free in Christ. Nowhere are we instructed that Jesus must again deal with sin because we fail to walk by faith.

Sin was dealt with on the cross, but we receive forgiveness when we put our trust in Christ. Sin as a whole has already been paid through His atoning sacrifice. We commit sins when we trust in something other than God, but all sin has already been defeated through Christ. The sins we have committed as individuals are judged and removed through the defeat of sin where Jesus removed the curse and provided our reconciliation back to God.

---

[22] 1 Corinthians 15:22

People are judged for their sins because they are in Adam. This is why the Bible says that Jesus did not come into the world to condemn the world. Those who believe in Him escape condemnation, but those who don't believe are condemned, not because Jesus condemns them, but because they are already under condemnation.[23]

It's a false statement to say that Jesus must reapply the blood of His sacrifice each time we sin. According to the Bible, this was done once for all. Once. Not daily. Not each time we repent. Once for all. Let's look at a few passages that clarify this. Start with **Romans 6:10-11**

> [10] For *the death* that He died, He died to sin once for all; but *the life* that He lives, He lives to God.
> [11] Likewise you also, reckon yourselves to be dead indeed to sin, but alive to God in Christ Jesus our Lord.

This is easy to understand, for we all know that Jesus only died once. But what people don't understand is that we who are in Christ must reckon, or account, ourselves dead to sin. It's an act of faith. I believe that Jesus died for sin. I believe that I died with Him on the cross and my flesh was put to death in Him. Now I must also believe that I am dead to sin and alive to God in Christ. It's already an accomplished fact, whether I believe it or not. But when I account myself dead to sin and alive in Christ, I am putting my faith in Jesus' work and receiving this truth. I am entering the work of Christ where sin was already defeated on my behalf.

When the flesh draws me back into a worldly way of thinking and I commit sins, I look back to the cross where I was set at liberty from the flesh, sin, and its reigning power over my old life born through Adam. Because I believe, I account. I know I have new life, so I remind myself that sin no longer has dominion over me and I step away from a fleshly way of thinking and into spiritual mindedness given to me through Christ. Read Romans 8:6-17 for a full explanation.

---

[23] John 3:18

Let's go a little deeper by looking at the atonement Christ made for sin. First look at **Hebrews 7:25-27**

> [25] Therefore He is also able to save to the uttermost those who come to God through Him, since He always lives to make intercession for them.
> [26] For such a High Priest was fitting for us, *who is* holy, harmless, undefiled, separate from sinners, and has become higher than the heavens;
> [27] who does not need daily, as those high priests, to offer up sacrifices, first for His own sins and then for the people's, for this He did once for all when He offered up Himself.

Once again, the Bible reiterates His one-time offering of Himself, but adds another gem. He now saves us to the uttermost since He is always present to make intercession for us, those who have come to God through Him.

We'll dig into these passages later when we address the misconception of losing the atonement. The Bible is painting a perfect picture of how earthly ordinances were given to show us the pattern of what Christ would soon perform in heaven. Take special note of the phrase, "Once for all". We'll see this again regarding the applying of the blood of Christ in this passage from **Hebrews 9:11-12**

> [11] But Christ came *as* High Priest of the good things to come, with the greater and more perfect tabernacle not made with hands, that is, not of this creation.
> [12] Not with the blood of goats and calves, but with His own blood He entered the Most Holy Place once for all, having obtained eternal redemption.

In this passage we find the heart of complete (or total) forgiveness. It is a completed work – once for all. Christ entered into the Most Holy Place in heaven, applied the blood of His sacrifice for sin – all sin – once for all. Sin as a whole has now been atoned for, and we can then be forgiven of our individual sins.

We receive forgiveness when we come to God through Christ. We experience forgiveness when we put our trust in Christ, though the atonement was accomplished before we were even born.

Understanding Complete Forgiveness

In the Old Testament, the Bible says the people could not receive God's promise because of unbelief, even though the works were finished before the world was even founded.[24] They missed the promise because they didn't believe in God's work. It was already an accomplished fact, but until they had the faith to enter into that promise, it could not be received. In the same way, the sacrifice of Christ is an accomplished fact. All sin has been atoned for. Every person can be under that redemption, but it can only be received by faith.

Every person is already under condemnation through Adam, but look at **John 3:18**

> He who believes in Him is not condemned; but he who does not believe is condemned already, because he has not believed in the name of the only begotten Son of God.

Why are people condemned for sin? They are condemned already because they are born into a sin nature inherited from Adam. They merely choose to remain under that condemnation rather than trusting in the completed work of Christ. It is unbelief that causes them to remain under sin.

Just as the Children of Israel remained in the barren desert because they did not believe God, each person in life is given the call of redemption. All are invited into the promise of rest in Christ. Each person either believes and comes to God through Christ, or they disbelieve and remain in the desert of condemnation.

Once someone is in Christ, they are under His redemption. They are now under the atonement for sin that was applied in heaven once for all. There is no second atonement. There is no reapplication of the blood when we sin and repent. Sin, all sin, has been atoned for and is under the blood of Christ – period.

The Bible never speaks of reapplying the blood. Under the Old Testament covenant, the blood was reapplied yearly for the sins of the coming year. It was constantly applied because it served as a yearly reminder of sin and as a foreshadow of Christ's

---

[24] Hebrews 4:2-3

coming atonement. According to the Bible, the blood of the Old Testament sacrifices could never take away sins.[25] It was never intended to take away sin. The sacrifice was to point to Christ, and by faith, people obeyed the Old Covenant ordinances as they awaited God's redemption.

According to scripture, the Old Testament ordinance of sacrifice covered sin for the new year. Even in this we see the revelation of the New Testament forgiveness. The Old Covenant atonement for sin was not for the sins of the past year, but for the sin of the upcoming year. They were applying the blood to sins that had not yet been committed. It makes sense, for if someone under the Old Covenant died before they could make the atonement, would the people have had confidence in God's forgiveness? In the same way, Christ atones for sin – even though our transgressions were not yet committed.

Unlike the Old Covenant, in Christ sins are not merely covered, but they are taken out of the way. This is explained clearly in **Colossians 2:13-14**

> [13] And you, being dead in your trespasses and the uncircumcision of your flesh, He has made alive together with Him, having forgiven you all trespasses,
> [14] having wiped out the handwriting of requirements that was against us, which was contrary to us. And He has taken it out of the way, having nailed it to the cross.

Christ is our covering, and sin is no longer in the picture for the child of God. It isn't hidden or set aside. It is gone, never to be remembered. When you say, "Lord, remember when I did this sin?" God says, "What sin? That was crucified with Christ, buried, and is now taken out of the way." So now the real question is, do I believe or disbelieve God's declaration that sin is gone?

For the believer, the past is no more. Once Christ completed the work, the Old Covenant passed away, for there is no longer a need of the shadow once the One it pointed to arrived. At that point it became sin to keep the Old Covenant. To continue to make sacrifices was a denial of Christ.

---

[25] Hebrews 10:11

In the same way, to claim that Jesus' sacrifice needs to be reapplied each time we sin is a denial of the completed work of Christ. It is to say that Jesus' atonement is insufficient without us keeping an ordinance on our part. If sin can only be atoned if I do something, then I am denying the work of Christ. Faith is not acts of work on our part. Faith is putting our trust in what God has already done.

Let me reiterate this again. When the Bible says, "Jesus atoned for sin once for all," to then say, "The blood must be reapplied each time we sin," is a denial of Christ. The great irony is that we are sinning by claiming that something must be done a second time for our sin.

The only thing that can be done on our part is to believe on Christ. Consider the words of Jesus found in two important passages. First look at **John 3:36**
> "He who believes in the Son has everlasting life; and he who does not believe the Son shall not see life, but the wrath of God abides on him."

Just as we discussed earlier, faith is the only requirement. Even faith is not by human effort, for the Bible says that God deals us a measure of faith, and now He is asking us to receive His promise of salvation by faith. God is asking us to believe with the power He has given to us. So when we disbelieve, it is because we have cast aside the revelation of God given to us. He gives us the power to believe, invites us into the promise, and then rewards us for possessing what God has given. Then the only work is the work of God that we have received. Let's dig deeper. Look now at **John 6:28-29**
> [28] Then they said to Him, "What shall we do, that we may work the works of God?"
> [29] Jesus answered and said to them, "This is the work of God, that you believe in Him whom He sent."

What is the work of God according to Jesus? This is the work of God, that you believe in Christ. Nothing changes after we receive redemption. When we sin and blow it, how do we make it right? It's simple. We believe in Christ's work of redemption. The blood has already been applied and we receive God's works by faith.

When legalists came into the church of Galatia and began teaching people 'Jesus plus human effort', Paul rebuked them saying, "Are you so foolish, having begun in the Spirit, do you now think you are being perfected through the flesh?"[26] By faith they received Christ. They fell from grace by looking to something other than Christ. They were called to return their focus on God's grace and again walk by faith.

The same is true today. We receive Christ by faith and find redemption and forgiveness of sin. God has taken sin out of the way by nailing sin to the cross and we put our trust in His work and receive the gift of salvation. When we sin again, we still walk by faith, only now we should have an understanding of the grace by which we stand. We look back to the cross and by faith reckon ourselves dead to sin and believe God's promise that we are alive in Christ.

We are trusting in what Christ has already done, not trying to get Him to forgive us again. Begging God for forgiveness is to disbelieve in what Christ has already done. Instead of perpetually trying to keep laying the foundation of repentance, we should be trusting in what Christ has done and believing in that promise.

Rather than slinking away in shame when we realize we have sinned and hiding from God, understanding forgiveness gives us the confidence to get up and begin walking by faith again. Instead of cowering from God or wallowing in defeat, the man or woman of faith looks to the amazing work of Christ, thanks God for what has been done for them, and steps back into a life in the Spirit where victory is a guarantee.

A groveler remains in defeat, but a person who trusts in Christ rises up and lives like the person God has created them to be. Contrary to what is commonly taught, the Bible does not teach us to be in a constant state of begging for forgiveness. And this leads us into the subject of the next chapter – understanding 1 John 1:8, "If we confess our sins, He is faithful and just to forgive

---

[26] Galatians 3:3

our sins." In the next chapter we'll examine this passage in the context that clarifies what is being taught.

Discussion Questions

When you feel like God is disappointed in you, how does that affect how you relate to God?

When you sin, God invites you to trust in His forgiveness and His ability to empower you to overcome. How does that change how you view your relationship with God?

Why does the Bible say that Jesus condemned sin in the flesh on the cross, instead of saying Jesus deals with each one of our sins?

Why does the Bible tell us to reckon (or account) ourselves dead to sin but alive in Christ?

The Bible says that Jesus condemned sin in the flesh once for all. He offered Himself as a sacrifice to sin, once for all. He sprinkled His atoning blood on the altar in heaven, once for all. Why does the Bible put so much emphasis on 'once for all'?

Review Hebrews 9:11-12. Does Jesus have to reapply the blood of His sacrifice when we sin again?

Why does the Bible say that the yearly sacrifice of the Old Testament priest can never take away sin? What was the purpose of the sacrifice?

Why did Jesus' sacrifice do away with the Old Testament priesthood and sacrificial system?

In what way is the doctrine of continuous atonement (reapplying the blood) taking people back to the Old Covenant?

According to Jesus, how do we work the works of God? See John 6:29.

Confess and Forsake – What is the Bible Teaching?

Scriptures point to the Old Testament saints as our example for understanding faith in the New Testament.[27] Many parallels are veiled in the Old Testament that actually point to New Testament faith. The people who were led from slavery in Egypt to the Promise of God's rest are a picture for the New Testament Christian. The Bible says that the true promise is the rest we now have in Christ.

As we examine repentance and the Christian life, keep this example in mind. **Psalm 78:37-42** paints a beautiful picture of how God deals with His people – including us.

> [37] For their heart was not steadfast with Him, Nor were they faithful in His covenant.
> [38] But He, *being* full of compassion, forgave *their* iniquity, And did not destroy *them*. Yes, many a time He turned His anger away, And did not stir up all His wrath;
> [39] For He remembered that they *were but* flesh, A breath that passes away and does not come again.
> [40] How often they provoked Him in the wilderness, *And* grieved Him in the desert!
> [41] Yes, again and again they tempted God, And limited the Holy One of Israel.
> [42] They did not remember His power: The day when He redeemed them from the enemy,

The people were not faithful and sinned against God many times. God did not stir up His wrath, but had compassion and forgave them. He remembered that they were helpless people without understanding. God had performed many mighty works, but they didn't remember. God didn't punish them; however, they did miss the greatness of experiencing the fullness of God. Instead of demanding the people to grovel, God pitied them and

---

[27] 1 Corinthians 10:6 – 11, Hebrews 4:11

had compassion, knowing they were lacking in true understanding. And this was before the cross where sin was taken out of the way!

When we realize we have sinned, we naturally emerge from our failure with the expectation of wrath. Certainly God has to be standing over us with stirred up wrath, ready to punish our foolishness. Surely there has to be punishment for our sin, right?

And here lies the heart of confusion in the church. We are viewing ourselves through human eyes instead of God's call. Sin has already been punished and taken out of the way. Certainly we grieve the Holy Spirit when we live for the flesh. It is like a loving parent who wants to see their children prosper, but is constantly grieved when their child makes choices that are self-destructive. Being human, we run out of patience, but God never grows weary.

We'll talk about consequences in another chapter, but this chapter will focus on how we deal with sin. One of the great misunderstandings is that God measures our sins and when we do something really bad, God is really angry. Indeed God will correct our behavior for our good, but the truth is that everything done through human effort is sin.

Those who feed the poor by their own efforts are in just as much sin as those committing blatant sins. This is hard for us to comprehend because we have a performance based society. God is not performance based.

When men brought their good works to Jesus in Matthew 7:23, He called them workers of lawlessness. Good works done through the flesh is the act of mankind declaring his own righteousness apart from God. It is to reject the work of God and determine we can merit righteousness without Him.

Sin is work done through the flesh when we don't believe God can fulfill us, right the wrongs done to us, or provide for our needs. It is man declaring his independence from God because he knows better. At the heart of works by human effort and wrong-doings by human effort is the same principle. God is not trustworthy or sufficient. We don't need Him but will instead trust in our own actions.

Once we fully grasp the magnitude of sin, we recognize that we are incapable of becoming righteous. That is when we look to Him as our only source. It is also when we begin to realize that we cannot walk according to the flesh without producing sin. Whether it be good deeds to make ourselves right without God, or pursuing our lusts in order to obtain gratification in what opposes God, sin is still sin. The flesh is still flesh.

So the heart of the issue is that we are either walking in the Spirit or walking in the flesh. In the Spirit, we have no sin, for sin cannot be a part of the life we have in Christ. In the flesh, we cannot be righteous, for God will not accept the glory of the flesh as a partner of His glory.

When you fully grasp this truth, you will quit measuring your behavior, for anything not of God is of the flesh and part of a sinful fallen world. At the same time, we have this absolute promise from **Romans 8:1-2**

> [1] *There is* therefore now no condemnation to those who are in Christ Jesus, who do not walk according to the flesh, but according to the Spirit.
> [2] For the Law of the Spirit of life in Christ Jesus has made me free from the Law of sin and death.

Let me point out that the phrase "who do not walk according to the flesh, but according to the Spirit," is not in some of the older manuscripts. That's why the NASB, NIV, ESV, and several other translations do not include this phrase. Regardless of the translation you use, it's important to understand what is being said. The Bible is not saying that we don't have condemnation 'if' we walk in the Spirit.

Anyone in Christ is in the Spirit. This is why Galatians 5:25 says, "[If/Since] we live in the Spirit, let us also walk in the Spirit." The Greek word 'ei' in this context is not asking 'if', but is stating the fact 'if it's so'. This word is translated as: if, since, and you are. In this context, the statement is that since you live in the Spirit, you should also walk in the Spirit.

Confess and Forsake

In the same sense, Romans 8:1 above is making a statement, because you are in Christ, you have no condemnation. So even if the last phrase was part of the original biblical text, it is not putting a condition on condemnation other than being in Christ. Those who are in Christ have no condemnation, for He satisfied the wages of sin. It is for this reason we now walk according to the Spirit and not according to the flesh.

It is for this reason that the reader is reminded in Galatians of the same principle. Since our spiritual life is reality, we should be walking according to who we are and not who we were. The spiritual man is who we are. The flesh is contrary to our new nature. The Lord is calling you to turn from the old ways of thinking and to begin walking according to who you are now.

I am going to use a number of scriptures here. These passages, taken together, explain this principle clearly. In the Spirit, you cannot sin. In the flesh, you can do nothing but sin. Those who belong to Christ have been given the power to live in the Spirit, yet many do not understand this, so they allow their lives to be ruled by the flesh. Whether we realize it or not, if you have trusted in Christ and are born into God's Kingdom, you are in the Spirit. Look at **Romans 8:9**

> But you are not in the flesh but in the Spirit, if indeed the Spirit of God dwells in you. Now if anyone does not have the Spirit of Christ, he is not His.

If anyone is not a child of God, they cannot walk in the Spirit regardless of what they do. However, if someone is in Christ, they are in the Spirit even if they are not aware of this reality. This is explained further in **Galatians 5:16, 24-25**

> [16] I say then: Walk in the Spirit, and you shall not fulfill the lust of the flesh.
> ...
> [24] And those *who are* Christ's have crucified the flesh with its passions and desires.
> [25] If we live in the Spirit, let us also walk in the Spirit.

Notice the choice. Even if your life is in the Spirit, you have the option to walk in the Spirit or not. Those who are walking in the Spirit will not fulfill the lust of the flesh. It's a guarantee. This is how you overcome sin.

Your flesh has been crucified with Christ, past tense, and all its passions and desires are dead and buried. By faith, we must trust in God's call.

Walking in the Spirit is one of the most misunderstood truths of scripture. To walk in the Spirit is to walk by faith – trusting completely in the work of God. We believe God's word, trust in what He said, and walk expectantly in Him. I speak a lot on this topic in <u>The Victorious Christian Life</u>, so I won't rehash the details here.

The key to understand is that anything not from God is sin; anything provided through Christ is of the Spirit. Repentance is recognizing we are fleshly minded, and setting our minds on the Spirit by looking to the Lord for what we need – including mercy.

When we fail, God doesn't seethe with anger, but He stands with an outstretched hand saying, "This is the way, walk in it." He then leads us out of the failure of the flesh and into the victory of the Spirit. God knows we are short-sighted and easily distracted. Spiritual maturity emerges as we learn to stop trusting the flesh and learn to completely trust in the Lord and all He provides. We are incapable of arising to His perfection; therefore, He became our perfection. Now we are called to walk in Him. That is the perfect Christian life. We partake of His divine nature, and by this we receive perfection – His perfection.

Our goal is to be fully persuaded that He has given us all things pertaining to life and godliness by His divine power.[28] Until then, when we feel pressured or deprived, we tend to take our trust from God and put it in the flesh. Whether we are intentionally sinning or trying to do good, whatever is of the flesh is sin. And we know that flesh and blood cannot inherit the Kingdom of God.[29]

---

[28] 2 Peter 1:3
[29] 1 Corinthians 15:50

Confess and forsake

With the above understanding, let's visit an often misunderstood passage, **1 John 1:9-10**

> ⁹ If we confess our sins, He is faithful and just to forgive us *our* sins and to cleanse us from all unrighteousness.
>
> ¹⁰ If we say that we have not sinned, we make Him a liar, and His word is not in us.

Context is very important. At times, we also must understand the historical context as well as the context to the rest of scriptures. 1 John presents an interesting order of teaching. At the beginning of this letter of the Apostle John, he immediately goes into defending who the apostles knew Jesus to be. He was a real, physical person that they saw, heard, and touched. An interesting shift begins in chapter two. This chapter begins with the phrase, "My little children."

In chapter 1, sin is presented to an unbelieving crowd along with three main points. The first one is that Jesus was physically present. The second is that everyone has sinned. The third is that anyone who forsakes sin and trusts in Christ will have life.

In chapter one, the focus is on confessing sin and receiving Christ as Savior. In chapter two, the focus is on trusting in Christ, our Advocate.

Now let's consider the historical context in which this was written. Gnostic beliefs were spreading as a counterfeit to Christianity. There are specific Gnostic beliefs John is confronting in 1 John 1. First, the Gnostics took a little truth and turned it into superstition. They believed that anything physical was sin. They taught that anything in the physical world was evil; therefore they also taught that Jesus could not have come in the flesh. He was supposedly just a spirit and not God in the flesh.

Gnostics believed they were without sin. Through knowledge (or gnosis), they achieved a higher spirituality and were without sin. They were made perfect through knowledge and not through Christ. Even if they performed sinful acts, they compartmentalized their lives and thought the sin remained in the flesh but their mind was above it. Gnosticism taught there were no consequences to sin and they could do anything in their physical bodies as long as they didn't bring it into their spiritual minds. It was a teaching of self-deception, for all sin passes through the mind.

As you can see, there is some truth that they built doctrine around. As with all cults, a certain amount of accepted truth is presented to prospects in order to get people to receive the doctrines that are false. They took the apostle's teaching and made it into a man-centered religion.

John is pointing out that denying the physical life of Christ was outside the realm of Christianity. Since they claimed to be sinless, they were calling God a liar, for it is He who declared, "All have sinned." Finally, John is warning that unless they acknowledged their sin and need for Christ and put their trust in Him, they could not be saved.

This is the topic of 1 John 1. It is not a message to the Christian, but to the Gnostics coming into the church with their version of salvation by personal achievement through knowledge.

To confess and forsake sins as they seek salvation through Christ is a message to the unbeliever and not to the believer. How the believer approaches God and how the unbeliever approaches are completely different. The unbeliever comes to God as a sinner seeking mercy. They confess their sins and forsake their life in the flesh. They receive Christ and are born as a new creation and child of God. This is not how the Christian approaches God. They don't drag their sinful guilt to God for redemption, but approach with confidence because of their position in Christ. Look at **Hebrews 4:15-16**

> [15] For we do not have a High Priest who cannot sympathize with our weaknesses, but was in all *points* tempted as *we are,* yet without sin.
> [16] Let us therefore come boldly to the throne of grace, that we may obtain mercy and find grace to help in time of need.

Notice the context of this passage. It is written from the perspective of someone who has fallen in weakness. But the Bible doesn't say to confess, forsake, and seek permission to come back into God's presence. No, the child of God is *commanded* to come before the throne of grace with confidence, not fear. We can approach with confidence because Christ is our confidence. He knows our weakness and has mercy when we need it. Our need is the result of human weakness, not spiritual success.

This promise is to those who have need, for when we are seeing victory in our lives, we don't need to be reminded of our right to come to God's throne. Knowing that our enemy will throw guilt in our face, God continuously reminds us of our acceptance – even in the midst of our failure to walk in the Spirit. God reminds us to trust in Christ. He can identify with our weaknesses and through Him we are welcomed into the presence of God. Because we are completely accepted, the Lord delights in us as children and wants to give us mercy and grace.

And this is exactly what John describes in **1 John 2:1-2**

[1] My little children, these things I write to you, so that you may not sin. And if anyone sins, we have an Advocate with the Father, Jesus Christ the righteous.

[2] And He Himself is the propitiation for our sins, and not for ours only but also for the whole world.

No longer is the Bible addressing the unbelieving world (including the Gnostics), but is addressing the children of God. My little children clues us in on the shift of focus. The topic is still sin, but now the focus turns from the unbeliever to the child of God. To the children the message is, "If anyone sins, we have an Advocate with the Father." That advocate is Jesus Christ. He is righteous and became the payment for our sins. Now He stands to welcome us, just as described in Hebrews. Not only is He our High Priest, but He also is our legal defender. The justice for sin has been satisfied, and we now have confidence in His righteousness and in His payment for our sin.

Propitiation means, "One who stands in the place of judgment for another." Our sins have already been judged and we trust in what has already been done.

The goal is for us not to sin, but when we stand in the flesh, we will be weak and fall. Then we have the confidence that Jesus is our advocate, declaring us to be justified because of His own merits. He stood in our place, sin has been done away with, and we can have absolute confidence as we rejoice in God's mercy before the throne of grace.

So does this mean we refuse to acknowledge our sins? Should we still repent and confess, and ask the blood of Jesus to cover our sins and make us right with God?

No, and Yes. No, we do not ask God to cover us by the blood of Jesus. As we saw earlier, this was done once and for all. We are commanded to be confident in that completed work. We are commanded to be confident in God's presence. Most people don't realize that to grovel in fear and shame is a greater sin than the failure that caused us to be ashamed. If God has commanded us to be confident in what He accomplished, then we are rejecting His work when we receive shame instead of grace.

Confidence in mercy and grace is a command. God wants you to trust in His mercy and not your righteousness. Nor does He want you to trust in guilt, shame, or condemnation. Condemnation comes from the enemy. To believe the accuser (the devil) over God's declaration over you drives you into the mire of the flesh and causes you to turn your back on the God who loves you. He loves you passionately enough to stand in judgment for your sins.

Now for the 'Yes'. There is nothing wrong with being sorry for your sin. There is nothing wrong with acknowledging to God that you blew it. It only becomes disbelief when we stay there or take it to the point of laying again the foundation of repentance as if what Christ has accomplished and given to us wasn't enough.

If being right with God is dependent on your confession, then you are trusting in your methods and procedures and not in Christ. The Christian's confession should be to acknowledge we sinned and blew it, but then to stand on our trust in Christ's completed work and be thankful for the forgiveness we have already received. Yes, you are already forgiven before you even recognize your failure. As you focus on God's mercy and grace, you can't help but walk by faith. Then you'll experience His will and not your condemnation.

The sinner's confession is to confess sin and forsake. The Christian's confession is a profession of belief in what they have received from Christ. We confess His righteousness to be sufficient to overcome our flesh. We do not confess sin, but we do confess Christ.

While you are stuck in the mindset of repentance and confession in order to be right with God, you are creating a barrier between you and God's love. God's love is always there, but as long as your back is to it, that love is not reality in your eyes. If you believe your righteousness is needed then you will never experience the righteousness of Christ. The just shall live by faith.[30]

When you fully understand the truth that you are right with God because of what Christ has done and not because of anything you do or don't do, then when you blow it, there is no barrier to prevent true repentance. True repentance is recognizing you are in the flesh and trusting in God's work of the Spirit. When you walk by faith, you will recognize that God has already made you righteous in Christ before you were born and before you sinned, and then you confidently come before Him, rejoicing in the free grace He gives to any who have faith to receive it.

All God asks is for you to believe in His work. When you are confident that God has made you right, then sin cannot hold you down. You cannot remain distant in your walk with God. You will quickly recognize your flesh's deception and will return immediately to the life in the Spirit.

When you understand that you are always right with God, you will always be in communion with Him. And He will grow you into maturity where sin loses its appeal and the Spirit becomes the focus of your life.

That is life in the Spirit. When you sin, trust in what Christ has done. Do not let sin have dominion over you – even if that

---

[30] Habakkuk 2:4, Romans 1:17, Galatians 11:3, Hebrews 10:38

dominion is guilt or shame. Trust in the completed work of your Advocate and High Priest, Jesus Christ.

The Conviction of the Holy Spirit

Since we are on the topic of confession and forsaking, Let's look at another passage that is often misunderstood, but should point to our freedom and trust in Christ.

The word 'convict' is only used three times in the Bible. All three times it is related to those who are contrary to the gospel – the unredeemed person. This word is used in Titus 1:9 in regards to those who oppose the gospel. It's used in Jude 1:15 when Jesus returns to convict and execute judgment on this ungodly world. The third use is in John 16:8. This also is referring to the Holy Spirit convicting the world of sin, but people misunderstand this as conviction of the Christian. Let's dig in to **John 16:7-11**

> 7 "Nevertheless I tell you the truth. It is to your advantage that I go away; for if I do not go away, the Helper will not come to you; but if I depart, I will send Him to you.
> 8 "And when He has come, He will convict the world of sin, and of righteousness, and of judgment:
> 9 "of sin, because they do not believe in Me;
> 10 "of righteousness, because I go to My Father and you see Me no more;
> 11 "of judgment, because the ruler of this world is judged.

The first thing I would like to point out is that Jesus interprets verse 8 for us, so nothing is left for us to assume. Yet people ignore Jesus' interpretation and because of this, few understand what is being said.

Jesus is preparing His disciples for His crucifixion and departure. It is to their advantage that He goes away, for while His physical presence is the focus, the disciples will never receive the power of the Holy Spirit. The Kingdom of God is about to go from the mentoring relationship of Christ to the indwelling of the Holy Spirit within them. In John chapters 14-17 Jesus explains many things the Holy Spirit will do, including teaching them the word of God.

In the passage above, Jesus gives the three main roles of the Holy Spirit. He will convict the world of sin, of righteousness, and of judgment. Then Jesus interprets those three roles. Of sin, why? Because they do not believe in Me. The conviction of sin is to those who do not know Christ. The message to the disciples is that they are not left alone to teach the world of Christ. The Holy Spirit will reveal Christ and convict those who do not know Jesus of their sin so they will see the value of turning to Him for redemption. According to Jesus, this is not the conviction of sin in the believer's life.

I know, this statement raises a flurry of questions, but stick with this for a few minutes and it will be clear. Remember, we are accepting Jesus' interpretation, and since He is the Word made flesh, His interpretation is the only one that matters.

Any who do not know Christ are under condemnation. They are guilty of sin and the Spirit convicts them of that guilt. This is why people are either driven to the cross, or they rebel against God. Why does the atheist seethe with anger at the very presence of a cross, a nativity scene, a Bible, or any display that points to the Bible? They are under condemnation, and the Holy Spirit convicts the world of sin. Men who love darkness hate the light because it exposes the guilt they wish to hide.

The Bible says that there is no condemnation to those who are in Christ. Their sins have been paid under the sacrifice for sin by Christ. Our sin, all sin, has been taken out of the way – once and for all. Conviction is the declaration of guilt. In a legal court, someone isn't considered guilty until they are convicted.

Conviction means my actions have been tried, proven, and I am declared guilty. I would then stand as a condemned man, ready to have my judgment pronounced. How can I be convicted of sin if sin has been done away with in Christ?

Does this mean I can sin freely because all sin has been paid? Do you realize that the Apostle Paul was asked these same questions? Every time he explained our freedom, he always asked and answered the question he knew the reader would ask, "Does this mean we can sin?" Look at **Romans 6:1-2**

[1] What shall we say then? Shall we continue in sin that grace may abound?
[2] Certainly not! How shall we who died to sin live any longer in it?

It's interesting that the same objections people raise today are the objections launched against the apostles at the birth of the church.

Read the book of Romans and see how sin is explained in the Christian's life. Sin is declared as dead and the believer is no longer under it. Each time sin is addressed, people naturally assumed the Bible was teaching freedom to sin. In reality, it is freedom to escape sin.

Notice the answer to the question above. Can we continue in sin? Certainly not! Did the Bible then say that sinning puts us back under condemnation? Did the Bible present rules to keep us out of sin? Did it say we had to lay again the foundation of repentance? No, the argument was rebutted with one simple truth, "How can you who have died to sin live any longer in it?" It's not the call to conviction and re-repentance. It's the reminder that we are no longer in that old life.

Romans above is in full agreement with Jesus' explanation of the Holy Spirit. The world is convicted of sin, but we are convicted of righteousness. The world is reminded of their condition of condemnation, but we are reminded of our righteousness in Christ.

Jesus said, "Of righteousness because I go to the Father." That is not a message of condemnation or conviction. If you want to use the word conviction, it must be this – the Holy Spirit convicts us of our righteousness. It's the reminder that we are no longer of the flesh but that we are the righteousness of Christ.

When we sin, the Holy Spirit within us brings to mind our righteousness and reminds us that Jesus is our advocate with the Father. Not only that, but He is our power to live according to the righteous nature God has placed within us. The Christian cannot live any longer in sin and be at peace, for when we are living contrary to our nature, there will always be internal conflict.

Understanding our righteousness in Christ drives us out of sin and into the reality of walking in the Spirit. Certainly, when we sin, we feel badly. This is because we feel the grieving of the Holy Spirit and are going against the command not to cause Him grief by our actions.[31] When my actions are contrary to the new man I am in Christ, not only is the Spirit grieved, but my own spirit is grieved because my actions are in conflict with my new nature.

The solution is to turn from the flesh and begin walking by faith. First I have faith in the righteousness of Christ. The Spirit reminds me of my righteousness and I am drawn to walk in what I have been given. I then have faith in Christ's work of forgiveness. By faith, I have gratitude that my sin has been paid and that I have God's power to walk according to an eternal nature. Sin does not have dominion over me – even when I sin. Instead of groveling in my failure, I can rejoice in the victory Christ has given me. That is faith. Wallowing in guilt is not faith and is not of God.

Let's introduce the true source of condemnation in the Christian's life. Look at **Revelation 12:10**

> Then I heard a loud voice saying in heaven, "Now salvation, and strength, and the kingdom of our God, and the power of His Christ have come, for the accuser of our brethren, who accused them before our God day and night, has been cast down.

Satan is the accuser. Night and day he stands before heaven and proclaims our sins and failures. He points out every sin, failure, act of disbelief, and accuses us continually. He not only shoves failure in our face, but delights in pointing out our failure in heaven.

We have the assurance that for every accusation, Jesus stands as our advocate. Satan points out our failure, and Jesus declares our victory and innocence. Because we are in Him, we stand on His merits and not our own. Satan can only accuse us, but cannot convict us. His accusations are met with the cross, where all wickedness was disarmed and total triumph was accomplished.[32] Any who are in Christ, are free from the

---

[31] Ephesians 4:30
[32] Colossians 2:15

accusation of the devil and the conviction of sin. We cannot be convicted because we have already been declared as justified before God.

Since he can't convince heaven that we are sinners, he turns to our emotions. He convinces us that we are sinners. He does this by turning our focus off of Christ and onto ourselves. Any who look at their own failures feel Satan's condemnation. What's more, he convinces you that his accusation is the conviction of the Holy Spirit. Then instead of faith, you have guilt. Instead of rejoicing in Christ, you feel that you must do something to regain your acceptance.

Because people don't believe Jesus' interpretation of His own words, pulpits all over the world are preaching that the Holy Spirit condemns you of sin and convicts you of the very thing Jesus has already acquitted you of. Churches and religion teaches people that Satan's condemnation is the work of the Holy Spirit, and this turns their focus away from Christ and back to the very sins Jesus took out of the way.

Instead of focusing on sin again, we should be getting off the ground and saying, "Thanks be to Christ for His amazing gift. I allowed my eyes to be drawn away, but the Holy Spirit has called me back into His victory. Even though I failed in my own strength, I am righteous in Him!"

Let me ask you this. Does feeling convicted have any lasting fruit? I have lived in that mindset for most of my Christian life. In the past, I felt convicted by the accuser's pointing finger. I didn't feel worthy to be in fellowship with God and it drove me away from Him. When I did enough repentance, I would begin to slowly feel accepted again – until I did something else wrong. Then the rollercoaster faith would start it's downward plummet.

Now that I understand that the Holy Spirit points me back to righteousness and calls me to stop looking at myself and my failure, but to Christ and His victory, sin no longer drags me into defeat. Sin loses its grip on my life. It's ironic that when I trusted in conviction of sin, I sinned more. This is because I was focused on myself and my actions. Now that my focus is on Christ, even when I sin, it's a short-lived defeat. Because my focus is on the gift of grace in Christ, I'm no longer drawn to dwell in a fleshly mindset.

Focus on Christ. Rejoice in His victory. Trust in His completed work. Turn away from the accuser and trust in the Holy Spirit's call to remember your righteousness. Christ is your victory and sin is defeated, paid, and taken out of the way. A Christian can't be convicted, for we are no longer under the condemnation of sin.

Discussion Questions

Which is the greater sin - to declare ourselves righteous by our own acts apart from God? Or to pursue our lusts because we don't believe God's promise to satisfy us?

Who is in the Spirit?

What is the difference between being in the Spirit and walking according to the Spirit?

In 1 John, is John addressing a different audience in chapter two than he's addressing in chapter one?

If the 1 John 1 is written to the unbeliever, how does that affect the way we interpret and apply what is taught in this chapter?

What does it mean to come boldly before the throne of grace? What do we receive and why?

Read John 16:7-11. According to Jesus' interpretation, who is the focus of each conviction of the Holy Spirit?

Define the word conviction?

Can a person who is justified by faith be convicted of sin? Why or why not?

Why is a person not guilty of sin?

Does my failure overthrow the work of Christ?

No more sacrifice for Sin

In this chapter we'll explore a passage that distresses many Christians – the willful sin warned of in Hebrews 10. Over the years, I have heard many explanations on this passage, but not one satisfied me. I have always felt people were either dancing around the text, or explaining it away.

The problem with this passage from Hebrews is that it's contrary to our established belief systems. When the text states something contrary to what we have always been taught, the natural tendency is to explain it away. "This isn't really those who have believed," is usually the explanation. Those who believe in perpetual repentance say, "This proves we lose salvation."

Both sides end up in a quandary. If sinning nullifies salvation, according to the below passage, there is no more sacrifice for sin. If these are unbelievers, why does it say "If we sin willfully after we have received the knowledge of the truth?"

The use of 'we' is this apostle identifying himself as one of those who have received, and it cannot be said that the unbeliever has received this knowledge. It's odd that on one hand people state the qualification of salvation, but when the Bible identifies the same evidences in those who turn from Christ, people tend to explain it away as though the unbeliever can trust in Christ but not 'really' become a Christian. Take the scripture at its word, and adjust your understanding to the word, but don't redefine the word to fit your beliefs.

As Christians, we need to have a clear understanding of these things so we are not tossed back and forth by every wind of doctrine. If you take away your preconceived notions and remove the denominational blinders, the meaning of this passage will be clear. And it will give you confidence instead of unfounded fears.

In order to understand Hebrews 10, it is vital to look at it in the context of the entire book of Hebrews. I'll begin by summarizing each chapter of Hebrews. You may find these overviews interesting and enlightening, but if not, feel free to skip past them to the conclusion. However, I believe you will miss the big picture view unless you understand the entire context of this wonderful book. With that being said, look at the controversial passage of **Hebrews 10:26-29**

> ²⁶ For if we sin willfully after we have received the knowledge of the truth, there no longer remains a sacrifice for sins,
> ²⁷ but a certain fearful expectation of judgment, and fiery indignation which will devour the adversaries.
> ²⁸ Anyone who has rejected Moses' law dies without mercy on *the testimony of* two or three witnesses.
> ²⁹ Of how much worse punishment, do you suppose, will he be thought worthy who has trampled the Son of God underfoot, counted the blood of the covenant by which he was sanctified a common thing, and insulted the Spirit of grace?

Few passages have distressed Christians more than this one. This is a great example of why context is important. If you have been around solid biblical teaching, you have likely heard it said that scripture should be viewed in context in order to accurately understand its meaning. Nowhere is this more true than in Hebrews 10:26.

Before we examine this group of verses in their proper context, let's look at the concept of sin as it pertains to the common but flawed interpretation of this passage.

It is often taught that willful sins are not forgiven. Once someone is a Christian, they no longer are excusable for willingly sinning. One man explained his view this way, "God gives us a one-time pardon. After that, we are held accountable for our sins."

Whenever complete forgiveness and God's completed work of grace is taught, this passage inevitably comes up as something that sheds doubt on our consistent right relationship with God.

Sin, by definition, is always willful. Sin is when my will misses the mark of conforming to God's will and commands. God says, "Do not lean on your own understanding," but my will causes me to choose my understanding over God's word. When I'm angry, I want to use harsh words or act selfishly. God's word says to answer with a gentle spirit. God says to love others as much as myself. Has anyone other than Christ ever accomplished this? To answer this, look in your closet. Do you have more clothes than the homeless? Do you eat only what is absolutely necessary so you can provide the poor with the same standard of living as you are experiencing?

If you ever act selfishly, disobey God, lash out in anger, fail to show love, or do any other thing or neglect anything that causes you to act contrary to God's command or nature, you have willfully sinned. Anytime you choose to act based on your own understanding, you have fallen into the common interpretation of Hebrews 10:26. In fact, since the Bible says that anything not done out of faith is sin, anytime we do anything without the full assurance we are receiving from God, we are in willful sin. That's what unbelief is. It is when our will either believes we know better or doesn't believe God is trustworthy. We all say we believe God is trustworthy, but if we truly believed, our lives would be a constant beacon of faith.

The truth is that all sin is willful. Sin is when our will causes us to act or not act according to God's will. If a willful sin could nullify the work of Christ, we are all doomed. Even to think upon sinful actions is a sin according to Jesus.

Consider how many times the Bible tells us how to deal with sin. In a previous chapter we looked at the words of 1 John, "If anyone sins, we have an Advocate with the Father, Jesus Christ the righteous." Consider another passage we also studied, **Hebrews 4:16**

> Let us therefore come boldly to the throne of grace, that we may obtain mercy and find grace to help in time of need.

The book of Hebrews has just explained that we have grace in our time of need and that the throne of grace is for those who need mercy. Mercy is for those who have sinned, not for those who are righteous. The perfect man or woman does not need to come confidently to the throne of grace to find help in the time of need. It's those who have failed that need help, mercy, and grace. And this is every person who has ever lived – Christian or unbeliever. All need both mercy and grace.

Let's look at another example. In 1 Corinthians 3:3, the people of the Corinthian church are called 'carnal', or fleshly minded. They were neglecting their spiritual life and pursuing the world. They were also condemned for being so self-centered that they were having wars and fightings among the members. They were even condemned for accepting one of the most immoral relationships possible – a man having an affair with his own mother. The people were strongly condemned for their ungodliness, but look at the declaration of the scripture in these passages:

> **1 Corinthians 3**:9 For we are God's fellow workers; you are God's field, *you are* God's building.
>
> **1 Corinthians 3:16-17**
> [16] Do you not know that you are the temple of God and *that* the Spirit of God dwells in you?
> [17] If anyone defiles the temple of God, God will destroy him. For the temple of God is holy, which *temple* you are.

Are there consequences to sin? Certainly. We'll dig more into that in a later chapter, but the important thing to note here is that even though these people were sinning, God still declared them as His field, His building, His temple, and His people.

The people are rebuked by saying, "Do you not know..." Eleven times in the two letters to the Corinthian church, they are asked, "Do you not know?" Reminding them of who they are was intended to shift their focus back to Christ. When you understand who you are and what Christ has given you, it changes the focus of life.

A person who understands they are forgiven and right with God regardless of their performance and ability will see the clear invitation to walk with God. The person who understands their status in Christ will be more apt to walk like who they are than the one who still believes they are bound to a fallen nature. A person who understands God's love will turn to Him when they fail, but a person focused on the perceived anger of God will not.

Certainly there will be those who shun the gift of grace and intimacy with God, but revamping the gospel to control people is not the answer. We can't strip away our freedom in Christ in order to control those who look at grace as an excuse to serve the flesh. If someone walks away from grace, legalism will not change their heart.

Manipulating people into submission by fear does not create people of faith. According to the Bible, it is the goodness of God that leads us to repentance.[33] True faith sees the goodness of God and draws people to turn their minds from a worthless world to the eternal inheritance of God. Mere religion uses the fear of consequences to keep people in line, but God presents His faithfulness and calls any who will come to be a partaker of His nature. Only a partaker of Christ can truly have a changed life.

Understanding the Willful Sin

Let's zero in on the passages in question – **Hebrews 10:26-27**

> [26] For if we sin willfully after we have received the knowledge of the truth, there no longer remains a sacrifice for sins,
> [27] but a certain fearful expectation of judgment, and fiery indignation which will devour the adversaries.

As previously stated, all sin is willful and does not exclude us from Christ. If committing a willful sin doesn't nullify Christ's sacrifice, what is being said? Let's dig into the context of this passage – including the historical context. It is a letter to the Hebrews. The Hebrews are the Jewish people, and this letter was written specifically to a group of Jews that had become Christians.

The Jewish people were raised in the religious system of the Old Testament. In the Old Testament, God established the blood atonement sacrifice where a lamb or bull would be slain, and the blood of the animal would be sprinkled on the altar in the temple. It was a yearly reminder of sin. Once a year, the people would have to bring a spotless sacrifice to the priest, he would examine it for perfection and then slay it. The blood would then be taken by the High Priest and sprinkled on the mercy seat in the holiest place in the temple as an atonement for the coming year's sin.

---

[33] Romans 2:4

There is much more to the Old Testament Law, but this is the context Hebrews is coming from. The Old Testament sacrifice was a foreshadow of Christ. Jesus was the Lamb of God, and all the Old Testament sacrifices were actually pointing to Christ. Not one of the sins were paid, for Hebrews explains, "It is impossible for the blood of rams and bulls to take away sin."[34]

The book of Hebrews takes a systematic approach to explaining the sacrifice of Christ and its application to the Christian's life.

The early church faced heavy persecution from the Jews because they were no longer keeping the Old Testament but were looking solely to Christ. The Passover, where the sacrifice was made, was also the biggest celebration of the year for the Jews. Anyone who had become a Christian was immediately at odds with the culture of their heritage. There was a lot of pressure to continue the sacrifice of the Old Testament, even though the Bible says that Jesus did away with the sacrifice by becoming the offering for sin.[35]

The book of Hebrews systematically explains who Christ is, the purpose of the sacrifice, and how Jesus' sacrifice is the fulfillment of the Old Testament. Let's summarize the teaching of Hebrews. Before we can understand the meaning of the willful sin of Hebrews 10, we need to understand the logical explanation of the sufficiency of Christ through the entire book of Hebrews.

The church in Jerusalem is being presented with the call of God. That call is to abandon the old life they had been redeemed from and look to Christ alone. Obviously, it won't be possible to go verse-by-verse through Hebrews, so I'll summarize each chapter. I encourage you to read the book of Hebrews while considering that it was written to the Jews through the lens of the cross.

Chapter 1 explains who Jesus is. In times past, God spoke to His people through the prophets, but in these last days, God spoke through His Son, Jesus. Jesus is *the* revelation and the end

---

[34] Hebrews 10:4
[35] Hebrews 10:10

of God revealing His word through prophets. The chapter explains that He is God, exalted over all angels, and upholds all things by the word of His power. This is the first introduction to the truth that Jesus is the one who purged our sins.

Chapter 2 states that the world to come is subject to Christ and all things will be put under His feet. His purpose is to bring many sons to glory. That is us. He is faithful and has become our High Priest. By saying this, the Bible is declaring that the Jewish High Priest has been replaced by Christ.

Chapter 3 focuses on the truth that Jesus is greater than Moses. Moses was the one by which the Law was delivered, and the Jews considered Moses to be the greatest prophet. Hebrews makes the comparison that Moses shared the house but Jesus is the builder of that house. The one who built the house is greater than Moses, who lived in the house (God's temple) but wasn't the one who created it. Jesus is that Creator.

Chapter 3 concludes by pointing to the children of God who rebelled against God in the wilderness. They did not trust in God's rest; therefore, they could not receive God's promise. The same is true for any who are unwilling to trust in the finished work of Christ today.

Chapter 4 explains that the Old Testament children of God were examples for us, and that the promise they sought is symbolic of the true promise of rest in Christ. It pointed to Christ and He is that rest and God's promise to us. The Law cannot give the promise, but could only take the children to the edge of the promise where they could enter by faith in Christ. Now that Christ has come, we enter through Him. Hebrews warns all to be diligent to enter through faith in Him so we don't miss the promise – as the Old Testament saints did.

Chapter 4 ends with the reiteration of Jesus being our High Priest and that we must hold to our confession – that Jesus is Lord and is our salvation. It ends with the promise that anyone needing mercy has the confidence of being welcomed before God because they are in Christ.

Chapter 5 explains how Jesus eliminated the role of an earthly High Priest when God made the declaration to His Son, "You are a high priest forever." The Old Testament high priest had to first atone for his own sins before he could handle the sacrifice of the people, but Jesus, our new High Priest, had no sin, but instead offered Himself as the perfect and final sacrifice for sin.

Chapter 6 begins with explaining how these Jewish Christians were unable to become teachers to others because they were stuck in a mindset of perpetual repentance. This was first mentioned at the end of chapter 5.[36]

The people were stuck in the repentance mindset because they were still looking at the Old Testament sacrifice – a sacrifice that was insufficient to take away sins. The old sacrifice had to be done continuously because it was a yearly ordinance. Once Jesus satisfied the Law and purged all sin, the perpetual ordinance was no longer valid. They could not go on to the deeper things of Christ because they were stuck on re-laying a weak foundation, and ignoring the eternal foundation that was already laid through Christ.

Chapter 6 goes on to explain the importance of growing into maturity by trusting in the promise. It ends with the assurance that because God cannot lie nor can He fail, they should be confident to lay hold of the promise before them (and us) knowing their (and our) souls are anchored in Christ. Again Hebrews reiterates that His priesthood endures forever, so we will never lose our confidence.

Chapter 7 explains the priesthood of Christ by comparing it to Melchizedek. Melchizedek was the appearance of Christ in the Old Testament. He met Abraham and blessed him. Because Abraham is the father of the Jewish nation, he is held in as high of a regard as Moses, but Hebrews says that the lesser (Abraham) was blessed by the greater (Melchizedek). Melchizedek did not have an earthly father or mother, nor did he have beginning of life or end of days. (See Hebrews 7:3).

---

[36] Hebrews 5:12-14

Chapter 7 has two main points. Christ is greater than Abraham, and His priesthood is the permanent replacement of the Old Testament priesthood.

Do you see a theme emerging? The old has passed away and all our focus should be on Christ. Those who are looking to the Law, that which has already been satisfied and replaced by faith in Christ, these people were missing the promise. They were pushing aside the eternal Christ for the earthly law that had already been replaced.

Chapter 8 gets into the heart of the teaching of Hebrews. It begins by explaining the purpose of the priesthood, and then explains why the first covenant needed to be replaced. The word 'covenant' means a contract with God. The Old Testament covenant was faulty because it depended upon man. The covenant itself was perfect, but in order to fulfill it, the covenant depended upon the perfection of man – which is impossible.

The truth is that the old covenant was intended to reveal the imperfection of man so we could recognize our need for Christ. Romans 8:3 also explains this – the weakness of the Law (old covenant) is the flesh. It is man's fleshly mind that is incapable of upholding God's perfect standard; therefore, once the old covenant failed through man, God brought in a better covenant that depended upon our perfect High Priest, Jesus Christ.

Chapter 9 explains the difference between the earthly and heavenly sanctuaries. The earthly was symbolic of the heavenly. This chapter explains that the true sanctuary is in heaven, and the mirage is the one on earth. The sacrifices on earth were symbolic of what pointed to Christ. Once Jesus performed the true sacrifice and made the atonement in heaven, the earthly sanctuary became obsolete. That which shadowed heaven was removed once the true sacrifice was revealed from heaven through Jesus Christ.

Chapter 9 asks the question, "If the earthly sacrifice purified the flesh temporarily, how much more shall the blood of Christ, through the eternal spirit, cleanse your conscience of dead works?"

This chapter concludes by explaining how the copy of the old covenant is no longer needed now that the true sacrifice from heaven itself has been offered. The old was a yearly reminder, but the new is permanent. We must now get out of the temporary mindset of a repeated sacrifice and put our confidence in the permanent sacrifice of Christ.

Chapter 10. Now we are leading up to the passage in question. Verse 18 is the climax of the argument, and verses 1-17 build up to that climax.

This chapter begins by reiterating the insufficiency of the animal sacrifices by again stressing to the reader that this is a yearly reminder and not the true atonement for sin. This is where we are told that animal sacrifices can never take away sin. Verses 8-10, Christ is the sacrifice and it was through his body that sin was removed once and for all.

Verses 11-18 reiterate the removal of the changing priesthood and the establishment of Christ, our High Priest. The Old Testament prophecy of Christ is recited and it's explained that this is the testimony of the Holy Spirit. Then the main point is explained, and this is the topic leading to the warning of the willful sin in verse 26. Look at **Hebrews 10:18**

> Now where there is remission of these, *there is* no longer an offering for sin.

Take special note of this truth. This is what the book of Hebrews is trying to get the Jewish Christians to understand. The Old Testament and the covenant that undergirded it has been replaced with Christ. It all pointed to Christ. It was the copy, or shadow, of the true. The true sacrifice and the true priest is Jesus Christ. Everything that came beforehand merely pointed to Him.

Now that Christ has been revealed, there is a remission of sin, and no longer an offering. The animal sacrifices are no longer an offering for sin, but a denial of the sacrifice of God through Christ. To hold to the shadow is to deny that Christ is what God provided as the real thing the shadow pointed to. Any sacrifice after Christ is not an offering to sin, but *is* sin, for it denies the completed work of Christ.

And this is the climax of the book of Hebrews and the main reason for that book of the Bible. Whether the reader is a Jew keeping the Old Testament or a Gentile trying to use their own ordinances, anything that denies Christ is sin.

From 10:19-26 Hebrews encourages the reader to have absolute confidence in Christ and to hold tightly to our confession of Christ. Now we have confidence because we are consecrated (or set apart) for Him, and we should draw near to God with full assurance. We no longer have an evil conscience, but we have been washed and purified. And what is that assurance? That we do something to keep ourselves right? No. Look at **Hebrews 10:23**

> Let us hold fast the confession of *our* hope without wavering, for He who promised *is* faithful.

We hold fast to our hope because God, who gave us the promise, is faithful. The Law failed because it was dependent upon man, but the promise of Christ cannot fail because it is dependent upon Christ. Anything that does not rest on that promise is rejecting God's gift and is also a denial of Christ.

The Willful Sin

This brings us to verse 26, probably the most feared verse in the Bible, "For if we sin willfully after we have received the knowledge of the truth, there no longer remains a sacrifice for sins."

What is the willful sin? It is to have the revelation of the truth that Christ is our perfect High Priest and the sacrifice for our sins, but then to deny His work and turn back to ordinances and depart from Christ. It is to reject what is in heaven and turn back to the failing earthly ordinances that depend on flawed man, and seek perfection through human effort. Hebrews is warning the Jewish Christians that if they turn from Christ and return to a religion that is once again dependent upon human effort, they are denying Christ.

Peter makes a similar point in **2 Peter 2:1-2, and 19-21**

> [1] But there were also false prophets among the people, even as there will be false teachers among you, who will secretly bring in destructive heresies, even denying the Lord who bought them, *and* bring on themselves swift destruction.
> [2] And many will follow their destructive ways, because of whom the way of truth will be blasphemed.
> ...
> [19] While they promise them liberty, they themselves are slaves of corruption; for by whom a person is overcome, by him also he is brought into bondage.
> [20] For if, after they have escaped the pollutions of the world through the knowledge of the Lord and Savior Jesus Christ, they are again entangled in them and overcome, the latter end is worse for them than the beginning.
> [21] For it would have been better for them not to have known the way of righteousness, than having known *it*, to turn from the holy commandment delivered to them.

And what is the holy commandment? Jesus said that unless people look to His sacrifice on the cross and believe that He is their redeemer, they will die in their sins.[37] The holy commandment is to believe on Christ – period. Not Jesus plus works. Not Jesus plus keeping the Law. Believe on Christ.

The message of 2 Peter is also warned about when the Apostle Paul is addressing the concern of a church that had been told the Day of the Lord had already come and they were left behind. In his explanation, the apostle adds information that applies to this discussion. Paul gives both an encouragement and a warning. Look at **2 Thessalonians 2:3**

> Let no one deceive you by any means; for *that Day will not come* unless the falling away comes first, and the man of sin is revealed, the son of perdition,

The term 'falling away' is translated from the Greek word, 'apostasia'. It means to forsake and turn away, or defect. A defector is someone who belongs to one nation, but defects by renouncing their citizenship in one country in order to be allied with the other. It's a willful defecting from the faith, not merely to

---

[37] John 8:23-32

fall into sin. It's just as we read in Hebrews – those who willfully sin by rejecting Christ's sacrifice are the focus of these passages. This is clearly explained in **Hebrews 10:38-39**

> [38] Now the just shall live by faith; But if *anyone* draws back, My soul has no pleasure in him."
>
> [39] But we are not of those who draw back to perdition, but of those who believe to the saving of the soul.

The word 'perdition' (Greek word apoleia) means, perishing, utter destruction, or ruin. It's the exact same word used in 2 Peter 2:2 above when it says 'destructive ways'. That word is also apoleia. This word is used to describe Judas as 'the son of perdition', and the antichrist as someone entering perdition (Revelation 17:8 and 17:11).

Chapter 10 of Hebrews is describing those who have received Christ, escaped from sin, received the heavenly gift, but then count His completed work as worthless. They then return to the flawed ordinances that could not take away sin. Since they are defecting from Christ and putting their trust in an insufficient religious system, they are drawing back into perdition and denying Christ. They are now putting their trust in man-made sacrifices and rejecting the Spirit of grace.[38]

This is also reiterated in **2 Timothy 2:12-13**

> [12] If we endure, We shall also reign with *Him*. If we deny *Him*, He also will deny us.
>
> [13] If we are faithless, He remains faithful; He cannot deny Himself.

Notice, God doesn't warn that He will deny us because of our lack of faith (which is sin). Jesus didn't even deny Peter after he denied three times that he even knew Jesus. Before the denial, Jesus said, "When you return to Me, strengthen your brethren."[39] After Peter denied Jesus, the Lord came and restored Him. The denial of Christ is not the weakness of our flesh, but to deny the completed work of Christ and His sufficiency to remove sin – all sin. One more passage reiterates this truth. Look at **Jude 1:4**

---

[38] Hebrews 10:29
[39] Luke 22:32

> For certain men have crept in unnoticed, who long ago were marked out for this condemnation, ungodly men, who turn the grace of our God into lewdness and deny the only Lord God and our Lord Jesus Christ.

At the heart of all of these passages is the same problem. The Hebrew church was being deceived into abandoning Christ and returning back to self-focused religion. Each of these apostles are addressing the same problem that will plague both the Jewish church in the first century, and the non-Jewish church in the last days. People who claim to be prophets or men of God will come in and teach that Christ is not sufficient. They will turn many to follow their destructive ways, deny grace or turn it into a lewd shadow of the true, and the way of truth will be blasphemed. Those who trust in Christ alone will be spoken against. In fact, the Bible says that those who trust in Christ will be called children of perdition by those who are in perdition.[40]

And this is where the word 'willingly' comes into focus. Many are deceived. Almost all of us have been taught legalism to some degree or another. Through ignorance, we think that our faith is dependent upon us, and this denies the power and sufficiency of Christ. Yet when we receive that knowledge of the truth, we escape corruption – especially the corruption of false religion.

The condemnation is to those who understand the completed work of Christ, but willfully put their trust in false teachers and their own works as they turn from trusting fully in Christ.

For you, the Christian reading this book, this should be both freeing and encouraging. God is not standing over you with a keen eye, waiting for you to 'willfully sin' so He can snatch salvation out of your life. God is teaching you that He is your sufficiency. You stand, not because of your ability to live up to the Christian life, but because He has the power to make you stand.

---

[40] Philippians 1:28

Do not be deceived by those who teach that you must do things, keep ordinances, or make up for your own wrongs. The message of scripture is to rest fully on the assurance that our promise is dependent on Christ alone. You are called to trust in Him, not yourself, religion, or any other ordinance dependent upon man.

Naturally, people ask if this means we do nothing? Yes and no. You can do nothing outside of Christ.[41] We can do nothing for God's Kingdom by human effort, but we become zealous for good works as we learn to abide in Christ. He leads us into the works He has prepared. Outside of Him, we can do nothing.

Before moving on, let's clarify one other thing. If someone falls into legalism, the Bible is not saying they cannot repent. Everyone struggles to get the human way of thinking out of their doctrinal beliefs. The flesh gravitates toward legalism because rules are viewed as a safety net and a way to fulfill human pride. When a person is self-focused, their desire is to feel they have accomplished religion. They feel that God owes them blessings or favor, not knowing that favor cannot be earned and God cannot be put into debt to us.

Spiritual maturity is the process of growing in the Spirit as we depart from fleshly ways of thinking. Legalism is of the flesh. Society gravitates toward rules. Just look at our legal system. Each year the rules expand and create more requirements. The education system gravitates toward rules. The same is true for the corporate world. Name any organization and rules keep growing over time. When a church falls into human understanding, legalism is always the result.

Read the book of Galatians. When the people were drawn back into the law, the Bible says, "You have fallen from grace." Yet this is not a fatalistic condemnation. It is a call to abandon trusting in old ordinances and return to trusting in Christ alone.

When Hebrews warns that there is no more sacrifice for sin, the warning is not a declaration of doom for those who have blown it. It's a reminder that since Jesus is the end of the sacrifice,

---

[41] John 15:5

any who look elsewhere must realize that there is no more sacrifice for sin. If Jesus was the final sacrifice, there remains no more sacrifice for sin; therefore, any who look to the old sacrificial system have no cleansing of sin, but can only expect fiery indignation. If the blood of animals cannot take away sin, and if someone trusts in that dead way of finding forgiveness, they don't find forgiveness but instead find a fruitless religious system that cannot cleanse their conscience.

There is a defecting from the faith, but it's also important to clarify that misunderstanding the scriptures and falling from grace into legalism is not unforgiveable. In fact, forgiveness has already been granted, but a person can choose to live according to the old life of condemnation and never experience the perfect fellowship that is within their grasp.

The bottom line is this: if you are trusting in Christ, the willful sin does not apply to you. This warning is only to those being tempted to put their trust in something other than Him. For those who hope in the Lord and trust in His completed work, none of these things are a concern.

Discussion Questions:

What type of sin is willful?

Why does the Bible call the Corinthian church carnal (or fleshly) but then identifies them as God's people and the temple of the Holy Spirit? Did their sins change their identity in Christ?

If someone is put into a position of persecution, and they deny their faith in Christ out of fear, is this unforgiveable? Does Jesus deny them?

If we put our trust on making ourselves righteous by keeping rules or the Old Testament Law, is that a denial of Christ?

Read 2 Corinthians 5:21 and Isaiah 61:10. If I believe my works make me righteous, am I denying Christ?

If I believe my sins overcome the righteousness of God, am I denying Christ?

What is the willful sin of Hebrews 10:26?

What's the difference between falling into sin and defecting from the faith?

Works – Stepping Beyond the Achievement Perspective

I want you to change the way you think about works. Instead of getting stuck in the human way of thinking of works as what you do for God, begin focusing in on the eternal view of works as what God is doing and inviting you to be a part of. The works of God are not dependent upon you. It is God working, and He invites any who will trust in Him to join Him in the eternal work He has done.

It is not that God needs you and I in order to accomplish His will. God desires to raise up godly men and women to share in His work so that they can share in the rewards of the kingdom.

It is not for God's benefit that we pray and do His works. It is for our benefit. God can fulfill His purposes without us, but then who would share in the joys of the kingdom? God didn't need man in order to create the universe. He didn't need our help to fashion the earth. He didn't ask for man's counsel when He built His purposes into the timeline of creation or prepared the works beforehand.

So why does God require mankind's involvement now? It is for no other purpose than for you and I to become partakers of His glory. Your call into good works is an act of God's grace. He calls you to good works because He favors you and wants you to be a part of what He is doing. Good works are not intended for you to earn anything, but for you to join God as a child works alongside their father.

To illustrate this, let me borrow from my book, The Victorious Christian Life.

I'm a gardener. My young children want to help Daddy plant in the garden. I don't need them in order to accomplish my work. I invite them to be a part of the work because I want to build that relationship. My younger children do a poor job. When we planted strawberries, they left the roots exposed. They were haphazard in their methods, but they had such joy in being a part of growing what would soon benefit us.

I went behind them and buried the roots, or rescued the plants that were buried too deep. Sometimes I prepared the rows and said, "Put a seed here, here, and here." Sometimes they succeeded, but most of the time they did not. But I made up for what they lacked.

When the fruit and vegetables produced, they helped me pick. They missed most of the beans and picked a few under-ripened tomatoes. I finished what they missed, but they were pleased to be part of what I was doing.

When they sat at the table, they looked at the fruit of their labors and were happy to enjoy what their work had produced. They got the benefit far beyond the value of their labor, but I didn't invite them because I wanted their labor. I invited them because I wanted them to enjoy growing. I knew they would feel special to be part of my garden. I knew they would put the strawberry on their plate and say, "I helped grow this." The food on the table had more value because they were part of its preparation.

This is what good works are all about. God doesn't need your labors. In fact, when you look to yourself as the source of labor, you are missing the heart of good works. It isn't intended to be labor, but fellowship. You have the amazing privilege of being a part of what God is doing. He is preparing His kingdom, and God has invited you to be a part of it.

When you fall short in your abilities, God doesn't look down and scold you. He embraces you as a child and approves of your desire to be a part of what He is doing. Your abilities are not needed. Your lack of ability is not a barrier, for it is God who works in you both to will and to do for His good pleasure (Philippians 2:13).

Looking to yourself misses the entire point. Good works are the pleasure of joining God as He builds His kingdom so you can enjoy both the experience, and have joy in the finished work.

Don't pollute God's works with human effort. Enjoy the fellowship! Good works are an act of God's grace to your benefit. He could fulfill the kingdom without you, but because He favors you, He invites you into His works.

God wants you to inherit the kingdom. He isn't standing afar off, watching men and women form their own ideas and rewarding those who figure out something that pleases Him. No, God is intimately involved in His church, that was purchased by His blood, and born through His Spirit. And His intention is to call you into His kingdom so you can have intimate fellowship with Him and be rewarded as if it were your work.

It is all of God, and even if we stumble through our labors and make mistakes, God is able to complete is work without the need for us to perform perfectly. Our Heavenly Father has no limitations and is able to correct any mistake we make. And we will make many. Most mistakes escape our notice because He steps in and perfects the work.

My early ministry provides a great example of this. When I first began life in ministry I preached a terrible message to a group of recovering addicts. At the time, I didn't recognize my failure, yet God entered into my flawed efforts and performed His eternal purpose. About a dozen people received Christ that day.

As a young preacher, I needed that encouragement. God cared enough for those people to reveal Himself to them even though my message was flawed. His Spirit was not. He cared enough about me to show His power to me in my works, knowing that it would be nearly a decade before I realized it wasn't my message that changed lives.

This is one of the mistakes I can clearly see. How many will I never see? The truth is, it doesn't matter, for it isn't my work that accomplishes God's eternal purposes. My best work can never accomplish anything eternal. The opposite is also true. My most feeble effort, if it is a work of faith in God's power, can accomplish wonders if God enters that work to accomplish His purpose.

When we trust in His works, we will experience His power. When we trust in our works, we limit His power in us. The one who is lifted with pride will be broken - not as punishment, but so we can see what true glory is. God uses failure to drive us into desperation for His power. The one stuck in human thinking will try to find ways around failure by appealing to human nature and searching for 'methods that work'. The one stuck in human nature will become discouraged and give up. Or they will fall back to methods that are limited to the success of the flesh.

The one who recognizes God's hand will see failure as their limitation and will begin looking to The Lord. God delights in using the person who humbles themselves before Him and has faith to trust in His power to accomplish His works. They recognize that what they do for God is temporal and will have no value beyond this life. This person also recognizes God's power to work within them to accomplish what their best efforts cannot. We must learn to understand that we can bring nothing to God. We are dependent upon Him for every spiritual thing and accomplishment. And He is the accomplisher, not us.

According to the Bible, God fully accomplished His works before the world was created. Let's examine a few passages that make this point clear. We'll begin with Hebrews. The Bible compares the Christian life (those who have received God's promise through Christ) with the Old Testament people (those who refused to trust in God's works). We are jumping into the end of this illustration, but look at **Hebrews 4:3**

> For we who have believed do enter that rest, as He has said: "So I swore in My wrath,`They shall not enter My rest,'" although the works were finished from the foundation of the world.

I want to focus in on the last part of this verse, "The works were finished from the foundation of the world." The people missed out on the benefit by not entering into God's work – which rests from human effort and trusts in God's divine work. The people were not asked to accomplish anything for God. They were asked to rest from their own labors and walk in God's works – works that were finished before the world was created.

This is beautifully explained in **Ephesians 2:8-10**

> [8] For by grace you have been saved through faith, and that not of yourselves; *it is* the gift of God,
> [9] not of works, lest anyone should boast.
> [10] For we are His workmanship, created in Christ Jesus for good works, which God prepared beforehand that we should walk in them.

Do you grasp the magnitude of this passage? You cannot be saved by works, for your works have no value in the spiritual world that will one day be revealed. The life we see will pass, for it is temporary, and that which is not seen will become visible, for it is eternal.[42] Add to this the teaching of Jesus on works in **John 6:63**

> It is the Spirit who gives life; the flesh profits nothing. The words that I speak to you are spirit, and *they* are life.

Anything accomplished by the flesh (human effort) profits nothing. Only the Spirit can produce the things that have life. Your efforts are bound to a temporary world and cannot pass into the eternal world to come. However, God invites you to enter into His eternal work so that you can receive the things that will remain when this life passes away. And God is not asking you to accomplish anything, for there is nothing you can accomplish. There is not any work you can do that can enter into the spiritual life of God's kingdom. You are bound to the physical, but God is not.

Notice the words above. You are created (your new spiritual life in Christ)[43] for the good works that God prepared beforehand. These are the works the Old Testament people missed, for they were focusing on their world instead of God's kingdom. In fact, when they realized they missed the promise, many of them decided to do God's work and take the promise by human effort. These were driven out of the Promised Land and many were destroyed by their enemies.[44]

Human effort cannot accomplish the work of God. Either God is leading us into His works, or we cannot enter. Period.

---

[42] 2 Corinthians 4:18
[43] 2 Corinthians 5:17
[44] Numbers 14:40-45

Either we answer God's invitation by faith, or we cannot enter. Period. Faith is always trusting in God's power, revelation, and gifts of His favor. Faith in ourselves is not of the Spirit and cannot put us into God's will. Working without faith is mere human effort.

In Christ, we are a new spiritual creation. As we learn to trust in Christ, we begin to see the path of good works that God calls us to walk in. Take note that the Bible does not tell us to make the good works, but to walk in what God has already made. This is missed by most Christians because a human-effort gospel is preached in most Christian circles.

Let me provide another illustration from my early church life. As a youth, my church began teaching on giving. They held up the testimony of a man who felt that God was calling him to give ninety-percent of his income to the Lord. He obeyed and God greatly blessed him. "Do you see what God did for this man?" the preacher said, "This is what God will do for you. You must give until it hurts."

Let me say first that I indeed believe that God called that man to give. God blessed because this man trusted in God's call. In the opposite way we see an example of God's power through the orphanage ministry of George Muller. His ministry was not on giving, but receiving. Muller felt called by God to completely trust in God's provision without having to ask for donations. He believed that God was leading him to trust, not beg. He had many struggles and times when he didn't know how he was going to pay the bills or buy food, but he saw the miraculous work of God in many unexpected ways. Muller stands as a testimony that God's call is trustworthy, even when circumstances would indicate otherwise.

History is sprinkled with people who abandoned all to trust the Lord. It's interesting to note that God rarely asks each person to trust in the same way. Some leave lucrative jobs and go into missions. Some keep lucrative jobs and give money. Some are everyday people trusting God to accomplish eternal things in their simple lives.

Jesus asked the rich young ruler to sell all he had and give to the poor, but He never asked such things from others. Jesus saw Matthew at the receipt of customs and said, "Follow me." Matthew left his life and job behind and followed Jesus. Yet when Jesus rescued the demon possessed man, He commanded him to stay. The once insane man stood in his right mind. Instead of praising Christ, the people asked Jesus to leave their coasts because they were afraid. The cured man begged to follow Jesus, but Jesus would not permit him to come, but said, "Go and tell your friends and family what God has done and the compassion He has had on you."[45]

Do you see that God's work in one person's life is not the call of God in the life of another? Who was called by God to accomplish His will? Matthew or the man set free from demonic possession? Both. One's calling was to leave all and follow. The other was called to stay and be a testimony to his friends and family. Neither man could adopt a different calling and stay in God's will.

To go when God calls you to stay is disobedience that cannot be blessed. To stay when the call is to go is disobedience that cannot be blessed.

It's important to learn to follow God's call for you and not His call for others. A great testimony should not be mistaken as a call for action on your part. It should inspire us to trust the Lord, but God determines the call. People who put God to the test without His calling will fall short, for they are serving God by human effort. Those who hear the call and refuse to trust, miss the glory of God that would have been revealed. Those who try to imitate someone else's call are equally in disobedience and should not expect God to bless. They will have turned faith into legalism, for human effort and man-made regulations have displaced the prompting of the Spirit.

To illustrate this, let's go back to the example from my youth. "Give until it hurts," was the message. In fact, I hear this echoed frequently from teachers and preachers; however, this

---

[45] Mark 5:1-19

cannot be found in the Bible. Abraham had great wealth, but did not give until it hurt. David had great wealth, and though he set aside gold and silver for the future temple, he also did not give until it hurt. The Apostle Paul did. He gave up everything for the sake of Christ. Yet the Bible does not point to Paul as any higher example of faith than Abraham or David. David is called the man after God's heart. Abraham is called the friend of God and the father of faith.

Abraham trusted God by receiving. The Apostle Paul trusted God by leaving everything behind. Both were obedient in their call. If Abraham had refused to receive, he would not have been living by faith. If Paul had focused on receiving, he would not have been living by faith. It is God who reveals His call and we who submit to His will. The focus is not on our works, but trusting in God's work. We must let go of what we think the call should be and trust in what God reveals to us. Anything else becomes a work of the flesh – regardless of what we sacrifice or what we accomplish in this life.

God may speak to your heart when you hear a testimony, and you may indeed feel the prompting to enter the same call. Yet I have met many Christians who are creating a false calling by an emotional compulsion or feelings of guilt. When we see the amazing work of God, the tempter may throw guilt upon you and say, "Why aren't you doing that?" Yet God doesn't measure faithfulness by accomplishments but by obedience by faith. Remember, someone had to be the tent peg holder for the Tabernacle of Testimony in the wilderness. Not everyone is called to be a Moses or Aaron. What's more, is that God rewards us for faith in His call. No one is rewarded based on their fame, recognition, or accomplishments. The work is God's and we are all part of the body of Christ. Each member's role is vital to the whole body.

I fell into this trap in my youth. Because of my ignorance of the word of God, I believed that I should give until it hurt. However, when works are by human effort and not by the call of

God, we become the ones who determine what is good works and what is not. And our perspective is flawed.

If I believe I make God proud when I do enough good works, then doesn't that mean I feel I've disappointed God if I don't do enough? And what is enough? In my case, I doubled my tithe. But it didn't hurt, for I could still afford to go to the movies. I upped my giving, but it still didn't hurt. I could still afford to go to a hamburger stand. I upped it more, but I still could afford gas for my car. How much would it take to hurt? How much sacrifice is enough? I was still living at home back then, so I knew I would not starve, even if I gave all my money away.

People praised me for 'being a giver'. I was accounted as spiritual by those in the church, but I felt like I was in bondage. I could not do enough to please God. It was as 1 Corinthians 13 states, "Even if I give my body to be burned as an offering, if I lack love (agape), it profits me nothing."

Wait a minute! Does that mean I can sacrifice everything, including my own life, for the sake of Christ and it means nothing? If I give until it hurts, it might still mean nothing? Yes, that is exactly what this means. I am not called to kill myself for God's kingdom. I am called to rest in the agape love of Christ, cease from my own labors, and walk in the works God has prepared for me to walk in.

If God calls me to give ninety percent, I can walk confidently because it is all His work and not my own. If I am called to leave my home behind and become a missionary, I can rest in Christ while I walk in His works to do ministry. If I am called to stay where I am and just influence my peers at work and live out my faith as a ministry to those around me, then I can rest and be confident in God's calling – regardless of what others are doing or telling me I should do. God has made the path of our works and He alone issues the call. Anything else is wasted labor by human effort. Any work, even that which is an offering to Christ, but is not God's move in my life, profits nothing.

Don't forget what Jesus explained in Matthew 7:22-23. Jesus tells about many who will present their good works to Him at the end of this life. They present many good deeds that they have done in Jesus' name. These works are things we all would acknowledge as good. Healing, feeding the poor, teaching the word of God, etc. These were done by well-intentioned people who served in the name of Jesus, but Jesus says, "Depart from Me, you are a worker of lawlessness. I never knew you."

How can good deeds done in Jesus name be a work of lawlessness? This completely dismantles the belief system of most Christians. The truth is that they did not seek to know Christ. They did not enter into His works. They sought their own efforts and never sought the righteousness of Christ. Or as the Apostle Paul said, "Seeking to establish their own righteousness, they did not find the righteousness of God."[46]

The truth is, God has already done the work. With or without you, His purposes will be accomplished. Or a better way of saying it might be, God has already accomplished His purposes. Let's look at another passage that illustrates this – **1 Peter 1:20-21**

> [20] He indeed was foreordained before the foundation of the world, but was manifest in these last times for you
> [21] who through Him believe in God, who raised Him from the dead and gave Him glory, so that your faith and hope are in God.

The work of Christ is reiterated in Revelation 13:8 when it says, "the Lamb was slain from the foundation of the world." How can God say that Jesus was slain for us before the world was founded? It's a great mystery to the human mind, but a great revelation to those who view life through the eyes of the Spirit. The fact is that God established His works completely, and then formed creation around His completed work. He wove creation into His good works and reveals these to any who will walk by faith. During the timeline of creation, God enters our realm to make His work manifest to those who walk by faith. He then asks us to walk in the works He reveals to us.

This is why Psalm 139:14-18 can say God saw us before we were formed, wrote our life into His book, and put so much

---

[46] Romans 10:3

thought into our life that it would be easier to number the sands of the sea than to count the number of His good thoughts toward us. Before we had a breath, our life was already written out. Before the earth was formed, Christ had already been slain for us. This was reality before time began, but was not revealed to us until God entered into time and space to reveal that work on the cross.

We are bound by time, but God holds time as an object in His hand. We receive God's works and promises when we trust in His works and not our own.

And here is another great mystery that's hard for people to comprehend but revealed to us by God's Spirit. The works were finished before time began, but we must believe in the works of Christ and enter by faith. We are not automatons. Just as the Old Testament saints could not receive the promise because they rejected faith, we also must enter by faith or miss the promise. God's works are an accomplished fact, but God has revealed them to us so we can enter by faith and walk in them. Or we can do as many before us – trust in our own works and only inherit the things of this life that are passing away.

Each day, as you seek the Lord, God enters time at the point where you are, invites you to trust Him, and calls you into His works so you can receive the reward of what He has done simply because you trusted enough to walk with Him.

Around you many voices are competing with His call. Temptation promises fulfillment outside of Christ. Jobs call us to devote ourselves beyond what is necessary. The world influences us to invest our lives in stuff and pleasures that are limited to this life only. Religion calls for us to work for God by our will and human effort. People invest their lives in activities that are not the calling of God. Sometimes people hear the call of God, but instead of looking to His works, they believe the false idea that we must do our own works for Him.

God is patient and works with us to reveal the truth of His purpose. Though we may falter, the person who trusts in Him cannot fail. Take to heart the words of **2 Peter 1:8, 10-11**

> ⁸ For if these things are yours and abound, *you* will be neither barren nor unfruitful in the knowledge of our Lord Jesus Christ.
> ¹⁰ Therefore, brethren, be even more diligent to make your call and election sure, for if you do these things you will never stumble;
> ¹¹ for so an entrance will be supplied to you abundantly into the everlasting kingdom of our Lord and Savior Jesus Christ.

Do you see the wonderful promises of this word? If these things are yours and abound in your life, you cannot be unfruitful. You cannot fail. You will never stumble. The gates of heaven will be thrown wide open to receive you. Isn't this an amazing promise?

The only thing required of you is to be diligent to make sure you follow the call and to receive from God so you abound in God's works. And this goes back to what we discussed in the first chapter – His divine power has given you *all* things pertaining to life and godliness. These things are already yours. Be diligent to not allow yourself to be drawn away from the surety of God's call. Be diligent to make sure you are not seeking your own works. Be diligent to receive all things He has given you.

When you are abounding in Christ, you have all things and the gates of heaven eagerly await to receive you. What a promise! This is the true message of works. Trust in God's works. Walk in what He has accomplished and is inviting you into. Don't allow yourself to come short in any gift. Do not allow yourself to be distracted from Christ.

The promise is yours. Abound in it.

Discussion Questions:

How can we rest from our labors and still do the good works of God?

Why does God call us into good works?

Read 1 Corinthians 1:27-29. Does God need talented and skilled people to accomplish His work?

Is your weakness a barrier to God?

Do you think God takes pleasure in using under-equipped people in His purposes?

Review Hebrews 4:3. When will God's works be finished?

How does this give us confidence when we are stepping out without knowing how we will succeed?

When you see a need, it's the call of God. Is this a true statement? Why or why not?

When we see the amazing faithfulness of God in someone's testimony, is that a call to action on our part? Explain.

If someone sacrifices and God blesses, in what way does this affect our calling by God?

Why are works an important part of the Christian's life?

No More Consciousness of Sin

Trusting in God's completed work of atonement is critical for the Christian life. We are called to rest in Christ, but in order to do this, sin must be completely eradicated from our focus. If you talk to most religious people, Christian or otherwise, they recognize flaws in their lives. Most are still aware of their sin and it creates a barrier between themselves and God. This is rightly so, for the Bible says that sin is the war of our flesh against God.

All sin falls into one of two categories. It is either a rebellion against God or disbelief in what God has declared. Sin is either declaring that God will not rule over us, or it is declaring that God is untrustworthy. Consider this passage from **Romans 14:23-24**

[22] Do you have faith? Have *it* to yourself before God. Happy *is* he who does not condemn himself in what he approves.

[23] But he who doubts is condemned if he eats, because *he does* not *eat* from faith; for whatever *is* not from faith is sin.

This is the conclusion of where the Bible discusses those who are caught up into rules and regulations, and these rules have neither merit with God nor a penalty against the Christian who doesn't fulfill these rules.

People are caught up into worrying about whether they are honoring the right days and holidays out of fear of falling out of a right relationship with God. Others are worried about eating defiled foods or not eating the right foods. This passage goes on to address those who are abstaining from wine or other drinks, or being condemned by those who see God's liberty and blessing in what they drink, but then reject those who don't share their expression of liberty. Those who abstain condemn those who believe in liberty. The Bible concludes the whole argument with one simple phrase, "Whatever is not from faith is sin."

Everything in life is either by faith or outside of faith. In faith, nothing is sin. Without faith, everything is sin. Period. Faith is the act of trusting God for everything. Clearly there are things that go against the character of God and we are commanded to not do these things. Those who do these are declaring that they do not believe the word of God. Yet even if we abstain from blatant sins, if we are not walking by faith, we are still walking in sin. Even the person who keeps all the rules of religion, but does not walk by faith, that person is tainted by sin. As the Bible declares, "All have sinned and fallen short of the glory of God."

Yet in Christ, sin has been taken out of the way and nailed to the cross. And this is where true Christianity parts with both religion and godlessness. Once sin has been taken out of the way, the perfect fellowship with God emerges, just as it was intended from the beginning.

According to the Bible, the Christian should completely lose all consciousness of sin. Does this sound odd to you? From the human perspective, this is hard to imagine, but we are not talking about your perfection, but the perfection of Christ that covers you. And this flies in the face of modern Christianity. I was raised in a traditional denomination where each Sunday was the proclamation of sin and the call for repentance. Sunday was the day of guilt, repentance, and confession.

Looking back I now see that not one person I knew walked in victory. There were people who put on a show of holiness, but when you got a glimpse behind the veil, they were no different than the rest of us. Sometimes conflict or the pressures of life brought out the worst ugliness from the people who appeared to be the most spiritual.

The truth is that any who stand upon their own merits cannot have victory and will not stand when life becomes bigger than they are. Yet any who truly finds freedom also finds victory. Faith cannot fail. Temptation in the Christian life is the luring of our focus away from Christ, and the enticement to trust in something other than Him. This includes trusting in our own righteousness, religion, or works.

One of the greatest temptations in the Christian's life is to be lured back into sin. By being lured into sin, I am not specifically referring to committing a sin, but the mindset of consciousness of sin. Because most Christians never understand that they are freed from sin – all sin, they live in bondage. Instead of learning to walk in victory, they are seeking a way of escape. They spend all their time under the burden of failure. God took the failure away when they trusted in Christ, but they have picked it back up and are needlessly carrying the weight of the world on their shoulders. Before we get into the passages that tell us about eliminating our consciousness of sin, let's first look at the elimination of sin as explained in **Romans 6:4-7**

> ⁴ Therefore we were buried with Him through baptism into death, that just as Christ was raised from the dead by the glory of the Father, even so we also should walk in newness of life.
> ⁵ For if we have been united together in the likeness of His death, certainly we also shall be *in the likeness* of *His* resurrection,
> ⁶ knowing this, that our old man was crucified with *Him,* that the body of sin might be done away with, that we should no longer be slaves of sin.
> ⁷ For he who has died has been freed from sin.

Anyone who is in Christ is a new creation. The old man (sinful nature) that once ruled their life is dead. He has been crucified with Christ. Has been, not will be. This is a truth that eluded me for more than two decades of my Christian life. I lived as though I were trying to defeat a sin nature, not knowing that it had already been defeated.

Let me give an example of what this passage is addressing. An elephant trainer once explained his methods of keeping elephants under control. The young elephant was tied to a strong tree. He could not pull free because he lacked the strength. Over time, he stopped pulling against the tree, knowing he could not break the rope, and certainly couldn't uproot the tree.

Once the elephant learned to quit pulling, the trainer would move the elephant to a strong pole in the ground. It would be difficult, but as the elephant grew, he could have pulled up the pole. But since he had been conditioned by the tree, when he felt resistance, he quit pulling against the pole.

In time the elephant was moved to a rod. The rod had no strength to restrain the massive elephant, but because he believed the rope bound him, he stood passively and waited without resistance. The rope had no power to hold him, but because he believed it did, the elephant submitted to its restraint.

This is what has happened to the Christian in bondage. The power of sin has been broken, but we are so conditioned to it that we believe in its power to bind us. It lures us and ties us to the temptation that overcomes us. We feel powerless to resist or break free, and because we are mentally bound to the lust of the flesh, we stand there helplessly until we give in to its demands.

You are not bound to sin or temptation, for he who is in Christ has been set free from sin. If you have trusted in Christ, your body of sin has been done away with and you are not bound to sin. It's time to start trusting in what God has declared and learning how to live according to your new nature in Christ as you pull free the ropes that once bound you to your old habits and lifestyle. You are already free. Now you need to believe and act according to who you now are.

Let's pull in a few more passages that explain our new nature. First look at **2 Corinthians 5:17**

> Therefore, if anyone *is* in Christ, *he is* a new creation; old things have passed away; behold, all things have become new.

In Christ, you are not the person you once were. That person died with Christ and you are a new creation. Not only are you a new creation, but that new nature God has given you is incorruptible because its life is in God and is a partaker of His divine nature. (See 2 Peter 1:3-4, Colossians 3:4, and Romans 14:4). The Bible says that we are in Him[47] and that in God there is no sin.[48] It's hard to understand these truths with the human mind, but by faith we must look at God's word and believe His

---

[47] 1 John 5:20
[48] 1 John 3:5

declaration. We walk, not based on what we feel, but according to what God has revealed to us. One of the things God has revealed is that He has given us a sinless and incorruptible nature. Let's review these two passages:

> **1 John 3:9** Whoever has been born of God does not sin, for His seed remains in him; and he cannot sin, because he has been born of God.
> **1 Peter 1:23** having been born again, not of corruptible seed but incorruptible, through the word of God which lives and abides forever,

According to scripture, God has declared that He has placed a new nature within you. It is born by the Spirit, it abides in Christ, has its life in God, and is incorruptible. And it cannot sin. This has to be true, otherwise when we sinned, our spirit would be corrupted and nothing corrupted by sin can inherit eternal life, for the wages of sin is death.[49] So what happens when you commit a sin? You stand by faith, you overcome by faith, and you must live by faith. Everything in the Christian life must be an act of faith, for only faith can walk in the Spirit where victory is an accomplished fact. Look at **Romans 6:11**

> Likewise you also, reckon yourselves to be dead indeed to sin, but alive to God in Christ Jesus our Lord.

By faith, I look back to the cross and reckon, or account myself dead to sin. It does not have dominion over me. I overcome by believing in the finished work of Christ and believe God's declaration that I am freed from that sin and alive in Christ. Contrary to what most churches believe and teach, the Bible does not teach perpetual repentance. I once taught this as well, but the Bible compelled me to believe God's declaration. Look now at **Hebrews 6:1-2**

> ¹ Therefore, leaving the discussion of the elementary *principles* of Christ, let us go on to perfection, not laying again the foundation of repentance from dead works and of faith toward God,
> ² of the doctrine of baptisms, of laying on of hands, of resurrection of the dead, and of eternal judgment.

---

[49] Romans 6:23

Most Christians never go on to perfection because they are stuck in the elementary world of constantly relaying the foundation of repentance, and they can never move beyond human weakness in order to receive the power of the Spirit. Constantly begging for forgiveness does not make you right with God. Believing what God has said and receiving His gift of life is what makes you right with God. And this happened at the moment you recognized your sin and received Christ. That is where repentance does its work. Once you are in Christ, the focus on sin is wiped away and new life becomes the focus.

Those who are constantly focusing on their sins cannot be focused on Christ. Not only that, perpetual repentance is a denial of the sufficiency of Christ.

There is a positive way of looking at repentance. The word repentance means to change one's mind. If you view repentance as recognizing you are focusing on something other than Christ and it reminds you to look back to Christ and believe His word, then that would be the right way of looking at repentance. However, if your focus is on bringing your sins to God and begging for forgiveness, i.e., laying the foundation of repentance over and over again, then you are declaring that you don't believe God's word. You are not believing God's declaration that Jesus sprinkled the Most Holy place in heaven once for all, but are instead asking God to reapply the blood.

If that is your prayer, it is a rejected prayer. A faithless prayer can never be according to God's will. God will NEVER reapply the blood. It is a completed work. Any teaching that denies this is denying Christ.

When your flesh overcomes you and your actions are contrary to who you are in Christ, what is the answer? It is to reckon or account yourself dead to sin. Step out of the sin, reckon that part of your old life as dead (which it is) and set your focus on the life you have in Christ. Understand that repentance is turning away from the flesh and back to your life in the Spirit, where you belong.

Sin shall not have dominion over you! Do you believe this? Until this is your confidence, you will have a faithless mindset that is ruled by sin. Yet when you believe what God has declared, God has promised to transform your behavior into the person you are in Christ.

If you get drunk, are you a drunkard? Not if you are in Christ. That drunkard is dead. Stop dragging the dead body of flesh around and acting like the dead man you once were. By the Spirit we put off the deeds of the old man. He is dead, but the deeds of the body must now be put to death with the old nature. In Christ you are sober and righteous. The inner man is incorruptible. You can't rise above sin by focusing on sin. An ex-drunk may fall, but he reminds himself of the victory he has been given, and begins to walk by faith in Christ.

Alcohol may call, but it has no power against anyone unless they turn back to the flesh. And a defeated Christian is someone who stays in the flesh as they wallow in remorse while trying to make up for loss through repentance, or by attempting to merit God's favor again. The same is true for those who fall to lust, greed, anger, or any other weakness of the flesh. Forget what is behind and turn back to faith in Christ. Live according to the new life He has given and the deeds of the body will fall away.

What was just stated will appall many Christians. It once would have appalled me, before I understood and believed the passages I've shared with you. Here's another secret for you to mull over. It isn't repentance that changes the life of people. It is focusing on Christ. God has declared, "My ways are higher than your ways and My thoughts higher than your thoughts."[50] God has also declared that the way of the cross is foolishness to those who don't believe, but to us it is the power of God.[51] The Bible also says that it is God who has compassion on us and subdues our sins.[52]

---

[50] Isaiah 55:9
[51] 1 Corinthians 1:18
[52] Micah 7:19

When you believe God and trust in His word, He steps in and does His work. Your iniquities will lose their power over you, not because of your self-control, but because God subdues your sins and empowers you to abide in Christ. The drunkard who stays focused on Christ cannot help but overcome. The same is true for any addictive behavior, negative attitude, damaged emotions, or anything that ensnares your soul. If you are depending upon repentance, your efforts are the only power you have. However, if you become Christ focused, His power is unlimited, and you will lose all consciousness of sin.

Sin Conscious or Christ Conscious?

Up to this point, everything has focused on laying the foundation of forgiveness. If there is anything in this book I want you to get, this section is it. If you can understand this basic teaching, your spiritual life can do nothing other than grow into maturity.

In the Christian culture, overcoming sin is taught the opposite of what God has declared. We try to become righteous by what we do and not by faith in what Christ has done. We try to change our behavior by submitting our will to the flesh in the hopes that the flesh can accomplish something that is against its nature. The truth is that we put off the flesh and put our minds upon the Spirit. If we don't believe we are who God says we are, how can we expect to live according to that new nature?

If when we fail, we wallow in guilt and shame, how can we expect to separate ourselves from the deeds of the flesh? Let's visit the passage where the sacrifice of Christ is compared to the sacrifices of the Old Testament. There are a lot of life-changing truths here, so I want you to read these carefully without skipping over them. Begin with **Hebrews 10:1-3**

[1] For the Law, having a shadow of the good things to come, *and* not the very image of the things, can never with these same sacrifices, which they offer continually year by year, make those who approach perfect.
[2] For then would they not have ceased to be offered? For the worshipers, once purified, would have had no more consciousness of

sins.

³ But in those *sacrifices there is* a reminder of sins every year.

There is one key point I want you to keep in mind as we move ahead. If someone's sins were paid, they should have had no more consciousness of sin. If the animal sacrifice of the Old Testament could have taken away sin, they should have no longer been conscious of sin. Keep in mind that this was written about people just like you and I. After the sacrifice, they would have made mistakes and committed sins. Yet, if the sacrifice had been sufficient, they would not have been sin conscious.

The old sacrifice could never have made the individual perfect. A perfect sacrifice would take away sin and should also take away guilt and shame. The worshiper would then no longer be under the guilty conscience of sin. Don't let this slip far from your mind as we go on to read **Hebrews 10:17-23**

¹⁷ *then He adds,* "Their sins and their lawless deeds I will remember no more."

¹⁸ Now where there is remission of these, *there is* no longer an offering for sin.

¹⁹ Therefore, brethren, having boldness to enter the Holiest by the blood of Jesus,

²⁰ by a new and living way which He consecrated for us, through the veil, that is, His flesh,

²¹ and *having* a High Priest over the house of God,

²² let us draw near with a true heart in full assurance of faith, having our hearts sprinkled from an evil conscience and our bodies washed with pure water.

²³ Let us hold fast the confession of *our* hope without wavering, for He who promised *is* faithful.

Let me draw your focus to the end result of understanding the work of Christ. Let us draw near (to God) with full assurance of faith. Our hearts have been sprinkled with the blood of His sacrifice and purified from an evil conscience. The sprinkling is referring to the sacrifice of Christ that was done once for all.[53] Look how many times this passage tells us to be confident in this

---

[53] Hebrews 7:27, Hebrews 9:12, Hebrews 10:10, and Romans 6:10

sacrifice as we draw near to God. It's mentioned in verse 20, 22, and 23. Three times in this one passage we are told to be confident in this truth. Then it concludes by saying, "Hold fast to the confession of our hope without wavering." And why are we confident? Because Jesus is faithful and His work cannot fail. The only 'if' in this work is our faith in what He has done.

Sadly, we are told the opposite in most religious circles. We are taught we are not worthy. We are told to continuously lay the foundation of repentance so we can re-obtain this promise. Yet the focus of God's declaration is, "It is yours. Hold fast to it without wavering, for God, who gave this promise, is faithful." In other words, it is not dependent upon you or your abilities. We are depending on God and His promise. When you become sin-focused, you have let go of the promise of God and are now living by a performance-based religion. You are then trusting in yourself and not the power of God.

The sacrifice referred to in this passage is the New Covenant. In Matthew 26:28, Jesus said, "For this is My blood of the new covenant, which is shed for many for the remission of sins."

We are in that new covenant. And what is one of the key promises of the New Covenant? "Their sins and lawless deeds will I remember no more." The one who believes should hold to the confidence of our hope in Christ without wavering. The Law could not justify because people could not keep themselves in perfection. Now the weakness of the Law, our flesh, has been removed as a barrier and no longer can we fall short of the perfection of Christ. It is not based on our perfection, but God's promise. He is the guarantee of the New Covenant. His guarantee cannot fail even if we fall short. Look at **Romans 8:3**

> For what the law could not do in that it was weak through the flesh, God *did* by sending His own Son in the likeness of sinful flesh, on account of sin: He condemned sin in the flesh,

Don't lose this important point. The reason the Old Covenant couldn't succeed is because it was dependent upon people performing the work of God and remaining sinless. The weakness of the Law was the flesh – the people. They could not measure up. But in Christ, the weakness of the Law has been removed. No longer is your righteousness dependent upon you. It is dependent upon Christ. The New Covenant cannot fail because even when we fall short, Christ upholds the Law. He is our fulfillment, and we receive His works by faith. He, not you, is the guarantee of the New Covenant.

If you are in Christ, you are in the New Covenant and because sin has been taken out of the way, God does not remember them or take them to your account. They are forgiven AND removed. When did this happen? It happened on the cross. It does not happen when you confess. It does not happen each time you sin, grovel in guilt, and seek repentance. Repentance in the Christian life does not mean begging God for forgiveness. To do so would be to deny that Jesus has already paid your debt.

As stated previously, the word 'repentance' means to change the mind. It also means to change direction. Repentance is to acknowledge that we are sinning because we are walking in the flesh, so we change our minds away from the flesh and set our minds on the things of the Spirit. We change directions by stopping our pursuit of the flesh and begin walking in the fellowship we already have in the Spirit.

Forgiveness has already been granted. Stop groveling in the flesh and instead put your trust in what God has already done.

God saw your sins before you were born. He foreknew you and nailed your sins on the cross, regardless of how depraved they may be. He already knew them and paid the debt before you committed them. So why do you hide your head in shame? God has already lifted your head and seated you with Him at the table of fellowship. Stop crawling under the table and rejoice in who you are in Christ. This is not pride or arrogance. It is faith in God's power to defeat sin, bear your shame in His own body, and make you righteous by His power.

Don't deny God's power to overcome your weakness. Believe God and be accounted as righteous. It is an accomplished fact. All you must do is receive it by faith.

When you blow it, put your eyes on Christ. When guilt points an accusing finger at you, put your eyes on Christ. When shame tries to cover you, put your eyes on Christ and rejoice like the spotless bridegroom who is covered with the robe of God's righteousness. Rejoice like the spotless bride adorned with the jewels of Christ's glory.[54]

This is why there is no more consciousness of sin. Those under the Old Covenant had to be reminded each year of God's provision for sin, but could never rejoice in the realization of being fully redeemed because they were waiting for Christ. We have this amazing gift in our very grasp!

When you fully understand God's grace – unearned favor – you will no longer have a consciousness of sin, for you will be focused on the gift of righteousness you have received. Rather than constantly having to seek forgiveness, you will become Christ aware instead of sin-aware.

Adam and Eve were naked and unashamed when they were in fellowship with God. But they thought gaining the knowledge of good and evil would allow them to choose good. Instead that knowledge took their eyes off of God's righteousness, and their eyes were drawn to their inability to become righteous. They hid from God because they were sin-conscious. Since they were now self-focused, they were ashamed. Even before the fall, they were never able to live in complete perfection, but it didn't matter until they became sin-conscious.

In Christ, we have that curse reversed. Once again we have the freedom to be Christ-focused, and when we are, we lose the ability of being sin-aware. The knowledge of good and evil is put to death and we look to Christ as our only source. In Him, all things are good and the flesh loses its ability to lure us back into temptation. This is how we overcome sin.

Sin is the selfish cravings of the flesh that demands we turn our eyes back to ourselves and try to determine what is good and evil based on how it pleases the flesh. Walking in the Spirit is when we are looking to Christ for life, righteousness, holiness, our

---

[54] Isaiah 61:10-11

provision, and the one who satisfies us with the abundance of His goodness.

As you focus on Christ and the provision of His unending favor, the sins you committed fall from view, and guilt cannot be found, for there is no remembrance of sin. The sacrifice of Christ has satisfied justice and we are no longer aware of our shortcomings. They don't matter anyway, for faith is not what we do for God or our ability to measure up. Faith is trusting completely in Christ and knowing all things are of Him, by Him, and for Him.

Guilt and shame may rise up to distract us from our focus, but like all temptations, they fall away as we focus on Christ, the Author and Finisher of our faith. Whether our sins were committed yesterday, today, or the distant past, they have already been overcome by the blood of Christ and we overcome them by trusting in His power. How long ago or how recently we have fallen is irrelevant. We have overcome through Christ.

God has promised that we are changed into His likeness as we behold His glory. It isn't you who transforms your behavior. It is God's transformation power as you trust in Him. Believe and trust in His accomplished work. Then you have no more consciousness of sin, for you are abiding in the righteousness of Christ.

> Let me summarize this chapter with **Hebrews 9:12**
> Not with the blood of goats and calves, but with His own blood He entered the Most Holy Place once for all, having obtained eternal redemption.

The Bible is once again showing how the earthly ordinance served only to point us to the heavenly accomplishment of Christ. In the Old Testament, after the lamb was slain for the sin of the person, the earthly High Priest would go into the holiest place of the Jewish temple and sprinkle the altar with the blood. Once again I want to emphasize that this was a yearly reminder, for man's efforts can never take away sin. This had to be done every year of the person's life.

How many times does Jesus atone for our sin in heaven? He did this one time. Jesus entered into the holiest place of heaven and atoned for all sin. He did this once for all, having obtained eternal redemption for us. When does eternal end? It doesn't. The work of Christ was accomplished. It only had to be accomplished once, for His work is eternal and cannot be undone.

When you sin, the altar does not have to be sprinkled again with Christ's atoning blood. Forgiveness and redemption was accomplished once for all.

Do you have to be forgiven each time you sin? No. Redemption was accomplished once for all. If you had to be forgiven each time you sinned, then the blood would have to be applied over and over. Jesus doesn't get nailed to the cross for each sin or each sinner. It was one work, accomplished one time, for all sins and all people. Jesus never has to reapply the blood to the altar in heaven, for the Bible says, "He sprinkled the altar with His blood once for all."

Rest in what Christ has done and let the Spirit transform your outward life into His finished work.

The sacrifice of earthly ordinances could never take away sins, for the sacrifice was not sufficient. As the Bible states, it could never remove the sins, so the sacrifices could not remove the consciousness of sin. This is compared to Christ. His sacrifice was sufficient; therefore, any who truly understand and believe will no longer be conscious of sin. When we commit a sin, it is an act of the flesh and we are called to step out of the flesh and into the Spirit. Sin is disbelief in God's work or provision. We sin when we try to fulfill ourselves through human effort. But once we step back into the promise of God, sin-consciousness is gone and confidence in Christ is all we need.

Believe God's word and obey this command, "For we have become partakers of Christ if we hold the beginning of our confidence steadfast to the end."[55] Believe God's word and partake of His perfection. Refuse to re-adopt the flesh's focus on

---

[55] Hebrews 3:14

sin-consciousness. It has no place in the Spirit; therefore, it has no rightful place in the Christian's life.

Discussion Questions:

Why does the Bible say that whatever is not of faith is sin?

What if we are doing good works apart from trusting in Christ? Can our good works be considered sin by God? Explain.

Can you actively sin if you are looking to God as your provider and fulfiller?

What happened to your old sinful nature?

Can your new nature become corrupted by sin? Why or why not?

How does our faith overcome our sin?

What does it mean to reckon ourselves dead to sin? Or alive in Christ?

What was the weakness of the Old Covenant. Why did it fail?

What is the strength of the New Covenant?

Has our weakness changed? Has the focus of the Covenant changed?

If the reason the Old Testament saints remained conscious of sin was because the sacrifice was insufficient, what should happen to our conscience once we understand the sufficiency of Jesus' sacrifice?

When did Adam and Eve become sin-conscious?

In the quest to know good and evil, what did Adam and Eve discover?

Did they already have good? Where did they find good before the fall?

If Christ is the focus, what happens to our focus on evil?

The Life that Pleases God

If you ask people what kind of life pleases God, most answers will include some form of good works or religious activities. Some say to keep the Ten Commandments. Others say keep all God's commandments. Feed the poor, do random acts of kindness, give to the church, or read your Bible and pray.

The truth is profoundly more simple than all of these answers. Let's look at a passage that specifically states the only thing that makes it possible to please God – **Hebrews 11:6**
> But without faith *it is* impossible to please *Him*, for he who comes to God must believe that He is, and *that* He is a rewarder of those who diligently seek Him.

Meditate on this passage and think upon all the rich truths packed into these few words. This passage reveals both the pleasure of God and the rewards of man. And works are not even mentioned. Keeping the Law is not mentioned. Living out the Christian life is not mentioned. We are directed to two main points – believe God and seek Him.

The truth is that you have nothing to give God that He doesn't already possess. According to scripture, His works are already accomplished facts. Your money means nothing, for He owns the earth and all that is in it.[56] Your money is a provision from God. Even the Old Testament principle of the tithe reflects this truth. Look at **Genesis 28:22**
> "And this stone which I have set as a pillar shall be God's house, and of all that You give me I will surely give a tenth to You."

Giving is based on the fact that God has provided it all. Out of this understanding we are called to give according to what we have purposed in our heart.[57] The reward is not in doing, but believing. Those who get a glimpse of the provision of God also

---

[56] Psalm 24:1, Psalm 50:12, Psalm 89:11
[57] 2 Corinthians 9:7

understand that we succeed, not by what we do, but by pursuing the Lord with all our heart. When we understand that God has finished the work, we then know we must seek the Lord so He can establish us into His work.

People who bring their good works to God do not understand the greatness of God. Consider Cain and Able. If you are familiar with Genesis, you already know that Cain was the first murderer. Cain was a worker of the field. He worked hard, tilled the ground, produced fruit, and took pride in the works of his efforts. He took the best fruits of his labors and offered it to God. The Lord rejected the works and Cain's sacrifice. Why? He gave God his best, what more could be expected? He worked with dedication and sincerity, took the best fruit that any man has ever produced, and gave it to God, but was still rejected.

Able, on the other hand, presented a different sacrifice. He tended to cattle. God blessed the flock and Cain took what God had provided, and gave it back to God. It was as the statement above, "Of all you have given me, I am offering this portion back to you." The animal sacrificed by Able was God's provision, and it pointed directly to Christ and the future sacrifice of His offering on the cross.

This is the message of faith – we believe God and look expectantly to Him for everything. If there is one thing that sets the life in the Spirit apart from the one trying to live by human effort it's this, to recognize that everything comes from God and nothing comes from ourselves.

God wants you to receive. I'm not talking about the worldly focus of material prosperity, though God does indeed provide for our fleshly needs. Prosperity is not money. Prosperity is not possessions. Jesus made this plain when He said, "A man's life does not consist of the things he possesses."

If a Christian is trusting in riches, they should not be surprised if financial trouble plagues them. They can name and claim all they want, but God is not moved. They can give 90 percent of their income to God in the hopes of the so-called hundred-fold blessing. Again, God is not moved. Anytime you think God must respond to your efforts – even if you have faith in that effort – then you have stepped outside of grace and into a merit system. God does not honor the merit system, for we can never put the Lord into obligation to us.

When we trust in anything but Him, God will wean us off that dependence. If it's money, money will fail. Then we'll either grapple with desperation for money, or we will begin to let go of what God is removing and look to Him as the provider.

If you are dependent upon emotions, religious experiences, or any other thing, God will bring the circumstances in your life to wean you off dependence on personal experience so you look to Him. Everything in this life is passing away. God doesn't want your hope to pass with this life, but rather He wants you to have the joy of an unfailing hope. That hope can only be found in Him alone.

God wants you to prosper, and true prosperity is the riches of His grace. Any earthly outflow of that grace is to make both His love and power known, but they are never to become our dependence or confidence.

Without faith, trusting in God, we cannot please Him. The whole meaning of our life is to learn of Him, experience Him, and enjoy God. It is the Lord's desire for you to have absolute confidence and trust in Him without having to depend on what you can see through eyes of the flesh. For we walk by faith and not by sight.[58] This is where most Christians lose their way. Let's look at a few passages to get a better understanding. Start with **Hebrews 11:1**

> Now faith is the substance of things hoped for, the evidence of things not seen.

We've all heard this definition, but what is being said? The word 'substance' is the Greek word 'hupostasis', which means the undergirding, assurance, or foundation. Faith means we believe God with such assurance, we can do nothing but trust in Him. Our hope is not referring to 'I hope so' as if it's merely a wish. Hope in

---

[58] 2 Corinthians 5:7

the biblical sense is to have such confidence in God's promise that we rest everything upon it. And that is a key word – rest.

In 1 Peter 1:13, we are instructed to rest our hope fully upon God's grace. Think about the magnitude of that statement. The world strives for 'hope so', 'want to', and perceived needs. We rest. The confidence is that everything we need is such an assurance, that we rest in that hope knowing it is a reality. Some of that reality will be experienced here, but nothing compares to what will one day be revealed. Rest in hope. Rest in grace. That is when your life will have confidence and peace. Look at **Isaiah 26:3**

> You will keep *him* in perfect peace, *Whose* mind *is* stayed *on You*,
> Because he trusts in You.

What is perfect peace? Perfection is completeness. And the key to this promise is trusting in God. Our mind is always looking to Him as our provider, deliverer, and confidence. A man or woman at rest can have nothing but peace. The person at peace will have rest. Look now at **Romans 8:23-26**

> [23] Not only *that*, but we also who have the firstfruits of the Spirit, even we ourselves groan within ourselves, eagerly waiting for the adoption, the redemption of our body.
> [24] For we were saved in this hope, but hope that is seen is not hope; for why does one still hope for what he sees?
> [25] But if we hope for what we do not see, we eagerly wait for *it* with perseverance.
> [26] Likewise the Spirit also helps in our weaknesses. For we do not know what we should pray for as we ought, but the Spirit Himself makes intercession for us with groanings which cannot be uttered.

Our hope is not in what we can see. Anything that is seen is no longer hope, but reality. To the Christian, it's all reality, but as we walk by faith, God provides from the hope of His promise to the present need of our lives. And here is a bonus – nothing is dependent upon you. While we don't even know what to pray for or how to find God's will, His Spirit is working within us to pray on our behalf. While you may be thinking a need is one thing, God sees both the real need, and the right provision for that need.

When we box God into our perception of our needs, we are blinding ourselves to the provision of God.

We may not see how God is working, but we trust Him as He leads us into His ever unfolding promise.

Now let's talk about the Christian's needs. Everyone knows they need the things of this life in order to survive. Jesus addressed this in Luke 12:22-31 when He said, "Take no thought for food, clothing, your body, or your life in this world." The promise is that your Heavenly Father already knows your needs. The world seeks these things with anxious minds, but the Christian should trust in God's provision and take no thought for these. Not only should we not worry, we should not even make these things the focus. Look at **Luke 12:29**

> And do not seek what you should eat or what you should drink, nor have an anxious mind.

Don't seek our daily needs? Isn't that naïve? In the world's eyes, yes. We are called to focus on something completely different. Look now at **Luke 12:31**

> "But seek the kingdom of God, and all these things shall be added to you.

This is reiterated in **Matthew 6:33**
> But seek first the kingdom of God and His righteousness, and all these things shall be added to you.

The world is focused on surviving and obtaining that which is passing. We are told not to let our minds be distracted by these things. Sadly, the vast majority of Christians are so distracted by the cares of this life that they never see the grace of God all around them. We are to seek the greatness of the Kingdom and leave the necessities of life to God's care – for He is more trustworthy than your efforts.

Also notice that we are called to seek God's righteousness. We are not called to establish our own righteousness. We are not being called to make ourselves righteous, but to seek the righteousness that only comes from God.[59] Righteousness is a gift from God.[60] Any who seek to establish their own righteousness will miss the righteousness of God.[61] We seek the kingdom of God with expectation and receive both righteousness and all of God's provision.

God has already provided. People miss God's provision because they are stepping away from grace and pursuing the world. It may even be a religious world, but if it isn't God's provision, it's of the world.

Let's not overlook what it means to seek. Remember our earlier passage, God is the rewarder of those who diligently seek Him? Jesus is reiterating the same principle. Most people look at this passage as a call to works. Works are the natural outflow of a life that is filled with the Spirit, but this passage isn't saying this. Jesus is not saying, "Work to build up God's kingdom." Let's add another passage into the mix for clarification. Look at **Luke 17:20-21**

> [20] Now when He was asked by the Pharisees when the kingdom of God would come, He answered them and said, "The kingdom of God does not come with observation;
> [21] "nor will they say,'See here!' or`See there!' For indeed, the kingdom of God is within you."

The Bible makes it clear that one day the Kingdom of God will be sight and all things will be made new; however, for the Christian, we don't have to wait for that day to begin walking in new life. We are already there. Our spirit is already part of God's kingdom and if we walk in the Spirit, we can begin the reality of eternal life now.

The person who understands what it means to walk by faith and walk in the Spirit begins living according to the eternal life they have been given. They rest in the hope of all of God's promises, knowing He is to be the one concerned about the things of this life.

---

[59] Philippians 3:9, Romans 1:17
[60] Romans 5:17, 2 Corinthians 5:21
[61] Romans 10:3

Let me reiterate this important truth again. Seeking God's kingdom and righteousness does not mean we seek to build His kingdom or make ourselves righteous. It means that we seek the reality of what has already been given to us. God's righteousness is already yours. You cannot become righteous. You are already the righteousness of Christ. Consider **2 Corinthians 5:21**
> For He made Him who knew no sin *to be* sin for us, that we might become the righteousness of God in Him.

There are many passages that teach how we are made righteous through Christ. This goes even back to the Old Testament. Abraham was credited with God's righteousness because he believed God. King David wrote in Psalms, blessed is the one whom God imputes righteousness. In Isaiah we are told that we are covered with the robe of God's righteousness. Now that Christ has come, the New Testament is filled with these truths. Here is a great example that falls within the topic of this chapter, **1 Timothy 6:11**
> But you, O man of God, flee these things and pursue righteousness, godliness, faith, love, patience, gentleness.

Who is the man of God? The preacher? The prophet? Evangelists? No, we are all men and women of God. Anyone who is in Christ, male or female, is counted in this passage.[62] The verses before the above passage talks about the sins of the world, but you should flee those distractions and robbers of your inheritance, and pursue righteousness, godliness, faith, love, patience, and gentleness.

Did you notice that the command isn't to become these things, but to pursue them? These are all part of the kingdom and are already yours. Pursue them. Don't be distracted by the cares of this life, but stay focused on what has true value. These are treasures. Another great example is in **1 Corinthians 15:34**
> Awake to righteousness, and do not sin; for some do not have the knowledge of God. I speak *this* to your shame.

---

[62] Galatians 3:28

Very curious. The command is to awake to the reality of righteousness. The church of Corinth was very worldly and had lost their focus. Now they are being told, "Wake up and see what is before you. Wake up to righteousness." It's right before you also. Wake up and pursue it. Receive it. Trust in what God has provided. And notice the natural result of awakening to the reality of what we have in the Spirit, it eliminates sin. This passage doesn't say to stop sinning so they can be righteous. It is to awake to righteousness so they don't sin.

Righteousness is not the only thing we have through Christ. Every spiritual gift and eternal benefit has been given to us through the grace of God. The gifts of God are the outflow of grace, and God has promised that He won't withhold anything good from those who walk by faith.[63] Let's visit a wonderful passage from **Proverbs 2:6-13**

> [6] For the LORD gives wisdom; From His mouth *come* knowledge and understanding;
> [7] He stores up sound wisdom for the upright; *He is* a shield to those who walk uprightly;
> [8] He guards the paths of justice, And preserves the way of His saints.
> [9] Then you will understand righteousness and justice, Equity *and* every good path.
> [10] When wisdom enters your heart, And knowledge is pleasant to your soul,
> [11] Discretion will preserve you; Understanding will keep you,
> [12] To deliver you from the way of evil, From the man who speaks perverse things,
> [13] From those who leave the paths of uprightness To walk in the ways of darkness;

Wisdom, knowledge, and understanding are all gifts from the hand of the Lord. What's more, those gifts, when received, become the preservers of our way. It isn't us who become righteous, wise, or keep ourselves from the paths of sin. We are promised these benefits when the Spirit is working in our life.

God's wisdom and knowledge creates discretion so that we are preserved from sin and from making choices that will lead us

---

[63] Psalm 84:11

to harm. It is God's understanding, given to us, that keeps us focused on truth and prevents us from being led astray. The life that pleases God looks to Him for these things, receives them, and then walking in what God has given becomes the source for your right living.

This is why the Bible says to those who are lifted up with pride, "What do you have that you haven't received from God. Why then do you boast as though you have done it and not received it?"[64]

The reason Christians miss the mark is because they are trying to establish themselves rather than trusting in what God has established and provided. This is why the Bible says that those who are ignorant of God's righteousness seek to establish their own righteousness and miss the righteousness of God.[65]

Everything we need, we have. The fruit of the Spirit provides all the benefits of righteousness we desire: love, joy, peace, patience, kindness, goodness, faith, gentleness, and self-control. None of these are the products of your efforts. They are all products of the Spirit of God within you. If you lack these things it is because you are looking to something other than Christ and are ignorant of the righteousness of God.

Let's take a moment to revisit 2 Peter 1:3-4
[3] as His divine power has given to us all things that *pertain* to life and godliness, through the knowledge of Him who called us by glory and virtue,
[4] by which have been given to us exceedingly great and precious promises, that through these you may be partakers of the divine nature, having escaped the corruption *that is* in the world through lust.

I realize I use this passage often. This is because few passages explain life in the Spirit better than the above. When the Bible says we have received all things, what more do we need to do?

Let's look at the Greek definition of the word all. The word 'pas' means: all. In the English, it also means all. What part of all

---
[64] 1 Corinthians 4:7
[65] Romans 10:3

are we missing? He has given us ALL things that pertain to life and godliness. What is excluded? Life and godliness covers everything. Our physical life and our life in the Spirit, both are fully provided through Christ. We discover what has been given through the knowledge of Christ, but even if we are ignorant, it has still been provided by God, we just never learn to receive it.

We are partakers of God's divine nature. As we learn through seeking Him, we discover more and more that we had not previously discovered, and as we partake of His goodness, we experience the victorious Christian life. Let's wrap this chapter up with one more passage. Look at **Proverbs 3:5-6**

> [5] Trust in the LORD with all your heart, And lean not on your own understanding;
> [6] In all your ways acknowledge Him, And He shall direct your paths.

In this we see the promise, but also discover why we lack the promise. Those who trust in the Lord learn to acknowledge Him and see His leading hand. God directs the acknowledging heart of faith to the knowledge where they can partake of Him.

The person who tries to establish their own righteousness is not acknowledging the provision of God. The person who can't trust is focusing on their own understanding. But the person who trusts God and looks expectantly to Him for everything, experiences the revelation of God's nature. They then partake of what they have discovered and they experience this as part of their life.

It is not selfish to look to God for everything. It's faith. It's an acknowledgement that nothing good comes without His providing hand. It's to believe that God is. He is all of these things. And He is a rewarder of those who diligently seek Him.

God delights when you receive of His works, which He has completed and offered to you as the expression of His love. That is grace.

When you love someone deeply, everything you do for them is an expression of love. When someone receives your gift, it pleases you. What happens when someone doesn't receive it? It was still a gift, but you miss out on the pleasure of seeing them experience the gift. They miss out on the pleasure of experiencing your love. Some people reject gifts because they feel like they haven't earned it, but it isn't as valuable if they earn it. If someone doesn't love us in return, that gift also loses value. Forcing someone to take a gift they don't want can never produce love.

We are God's children. There is nothing we can do that would earn God's love. The only thing accomplished by refusing grace is closing the door to us experiencing God's perfect love. You are everything in Christ. The more you understand God's love and acceptance, the more valued grace becomes. You are righteous, holy, and perfected in Him. God wants nothing more than to experience the pleasure of you experiencing every perfect gift.

Once you understand that everything is a gift of God, then walking in grace will become a reality.

God is a rewarder of those who believe in who He is, and diligently seek Him. Without faith it is impossible to please God, but the person who has faith in who God is, and believes enough to receive all God has given, can do nothing but walk in a way that pleases God. And the person who walks by faith will always experience the transforming power of the Spirit. This is why right believing equals right living.

Discussion Questions:

Review Hebrews 11:6. Who is under the promise of God's reward? What role do works play in this promise?

Can we give anything to God that He has not first given us?

Does God need our labors?

Why did God reject Cain's works?

How can the Christian have peace when circumstances should make us anxious?

If our prayers fall short, how does the Holy Spirit help us?

How do we not have an anxious mind?

Why is God pleased when we trust in spite of hard circumstances?

What does it mean to become a partaker of God's divine nature?

Why is God more pleased when you receive grace than when you try to earn it?

What does it mean to acknowledge God in all your ways?

What is the life that pleases God?

Consequences of Sin

In previous chapters we've discussed how that living by faith naturally drives us out of sin, but this doesn't mean a Christian will never sin. We sin when our focus is drawn off of Christ and onto something other than Him. This could be a man-centered religion, or actively pursuing temptation.

Temptation is the promise of fulfillment in the flesh. The flesh never satisfies, but temptation does a good job of persuading us that it has something that can fulfill. Even the most spiritual Christian can be lured into a fleshly way of thinking. The Apostle Paul explained this in **Romans 7:23**

> But I see another law in my members, warring against the Law of my mind, and bringing me into captivity to the Law of sin which is in my members.

Even the apostles of Jesus were not immune to temptation. But look at the solution against temptation Paul explains in the next two verses. **Romans 7:24-25**

> [24] O wretched man that I am! Who will deliver me from this body of death?
> [25] I thank God-- through Jesus Christ our Lord! So then, with the mind I myself serve the Law of God, but with the flesh the Law of sin.

Notice that groveling in defeat is not the answer. Nor is trying to beg for forgiveness, doing works, re-laying the foundation of repentance, or any other effort. The answer is to thank God for our deliverance through Jesus Christ. When sin warred against Paul's mind and brought him into captivity, it was a distraction from Christ.

One of the great ironies in the church is the focus on sin and how it has the opposite effect. Each Sunday, lessons and sermons tell people to focus on their sins, seek forgiveness, and to relay the foundation of repentance. Yet as long as we are focused on sin, what are we not looking at? Christ.

Let's bring in a few scriptures that show us the transforming power of the life we have been given and see how it overcomes sin. First look at **2 Corinthians 3:18**

> But we all, with unveiled face, beholding as in a mirror the glory of the Lord, are being transformed into the same image from glory to glory, just as by the Spirit of the Lord.

How do we become like Christ? By examining our lives, looking for sin, and pleading for forgiveness? No. We are transformed into His glorious image as we behold His glory. The more focused you are on Christ, the more your life will conform to His image. This is reiterated in **Romans 12:2**

> And do not be conformed to this world, but be transformed by the renewing of your mind, that you may prove what *is* that good and acceptable and perfect will of God.

Once again, how are we transformed? Through repentance? Through focusing upon our sins and sorrowing over our failures? No, we are transformed as we renew our minds by focusing on the perfect will of God. And it is God's will – that you conform to the image of Christ.[66]

If your focus is on Christ and the completed works given to you, your life will begin transforming into His image. If you focus on sin and your failure, what will you transform into? Perpetual repentance has the opposite effect of what we desire. It takes our focus off of Christ and puts it onto ourselves. We then try to conform ourselves to God's image by human effort. We try to identify our sins, and by focusing on sin, we attempt to root it out of our lives. However, because sin and self is the focus, we remain in the flesh and cannot conform to anything but what our flesh has the power to do. And according to the Bible, "Who will rescue me from this body of death?" We can't rescue ourselves.

The answer for the Christian is the same answer given to Paul. Sin wars against us and tries to bring us into despair. Sooner or later we'll come to realize that we cannot overcome sin, and

---

[66] Romans 8:29-30

that is when we look away from ourselves for a better answer. The only true answer is, "I thank God through Christ."

When sin overcomes you, the answer is not to focus on the sins we have committed. The answer is to return our focus on Christ and rejoice in the deliverance we have already been given.

For the Christian, praying, "God forgive me," is a prayer of unbelief. The non-Christian prays this as they turn to Christ, but since we are already in Christ, the Bible says that sin has been done away with. Asking God to do something with our sin is an acknowledgement that we don't believe God's declaration of our forgiveness. The apostles didn't say that sin wars against our minds, and the answer is to seek a new gift of forgiveness. No, the answer is to rejoice in our forgiveness and believe in what Christ has done.

Sin no longer has dominion over us, and once we recognize its attempt to regain a stronghold in our minds, the command of scripture is, "Reckon yourself dead indeed to sin but alive in Christ."[67] Praying for God to reapply the blood is to say we don't believe Jesus did this once for all as the Bible says. Praying for re-forgiveness is to say we don't believe we have been forgiven.

When we sin, we turn from that sin, thank God for rescuing us from the body of sin, and begin walking in the new life we have been given. We not only reckon (or account) ourselves dead to sin, but also alive in Christ. It's a command to overcome by believing that we have been delivered from the flesh, and to trust in the life we have from the Spirit. We step out of the dead works of the flesh, and into the new life of the Spirit.

As stated earlier, when we trust in God's work, we also begin to see that sin is incompatible with our life. The Holy Spirit convicts us of righteousness by showing us who we are in Christ, and this makes it impossible to be comfortable in sin. Christians indeed commit sins, but because we have the Holy Spirit within us, we can never be at ease in sin. Nor can we ever be at peace through perpetual repentance. The person who keeps asking God to do what has already been done is living just as much in the

---

[67] Romans 6:11

flesh as those who actively sin. There can be no peace or victory because we are walking contrary to who we are in Christ.

This is why people repent every week but never get to the point where they feel truly accepted by God. As long as they are looking at themselves, they can never rest in Christ. The person who understands the completed work of Christ has peace and rest because they are not trusting in their abilities, but in Christ. And as we trust, we receive. As we receive, we discover the promise, "To him who has, more will be given."[68] The more we receive from God, the more we discover His will and how much He desires to bring into our lives. The fruit of the Spirit is the work of God and not the work of personal effort.

Wallowing in guilt is a subtle form of self-love. It is to pay homage to our emotions as though they must be appeased before we can receive acceptance. The Bible says that we love God in response to God's great love expressed toward us, but when our affections are stuck on the flesh, we are blind to God's love. Serving feelings causes us to trust in the flesh instead of in the love of God.

Receiving God's acceptance is to declare our trust in God's power to overcome the weakness of our flesh. It is also to believe His declaration that He loves us because we are His, and not because we have earned favor. Love cannot exist in a merit system. God's love casts out all fear, for instead of thinking we are rejected because of our weaknesses, we understand God cares enough to subdue our weaknesses and establish us in His righteousness.

Understanding this causes us to trust in God's love instead of our own worthiness.

The Carnal Christian

While it is true that our sins have been dealt with, there are still consequences to living for this life only. Sin is choosing our

---

[68] Matthew 13:12

will over God's will. Keep in mind that God is working in our lives according to the eternal perspective. Anything that is focused on the world that is passing away is a carnal (or fleshly) way of living. Never lose sight of Jesus' words, "It's the Father's good pleasure to give you the Kingdom."

The Kingdom of God is eternal, and everything in the Christian life should be lived through trusting in God's eternal perspective. Take to heart **2 Corinthians 4:18**

> While we do not look at the things which are seen, but at the things which are not seen. For the things which are seen *are* temporary, but the things which are not seen *are* eternal.

Even the Christian has to live in a temporal world, but we don't live *for* this temporal world. Nor do we seek pleasure in the lusts of the world. Yet a Christian who focuses on this world can begin seeking fulfillment through the flesh and reject or neglect the life of the Spirit. In fact, most Christians live this way. God is constantly dealing with the Christian, but most view God's correction as a trial and never look to see if He's working to shift our focus off trusting in the world so we can find the true focus and meaning of life.

Sin emerges when we put our trust in the things of the flesh because we don't trust God. This is why the Bible says that an evil heart of unbelief is what causes us to depart from the ways of God.[69] Grace is often misrepresented as winking at sin, but there are indeed consequences. In the remainder of this chapter, we'll look at what the Bible teaches about the three ways sin affects the life of the Christian.

Christian Bondage

Sin is a slave master, and temptation is the bait to entrap us under its bondage. To the world, sin gives the illusion of freedom, but is anyone free? When someone casts off restraint, it feels like freedom for the moment; however, is there one example of a

---

[69] Hebrews 3:12

person living a sinful lifestyle that has peace, joy, or freedom? The consequences of sin are all around us. Temptation is bait on a hook. There is a moment of joy when someone takes the bait, but joy turns to despair when the consequences roll in. Consider the words of Jesus in **John 8:34-35**

> [34] Jesus answered them, "Most assuredly, I say to you, whoever commits sin is a slave of sin.
> [35] "And a slave does not abide in the house forever, *but* a son abides forever.

The people confronting Jesus in this passage claimed to be free and not in bondage to anyone. In reality they were enslaved, but were blind to their state. Most people are blind to their bondage until the ugly side of sin appears, and then they can't escape its dominion. It may come in the form of an addiction, consequences, depression, or any number of ways sin emerges in a life.

Those who have not been given a new spirit in Christ, can do nothing other than live according to a sin nature. Only a son of the Kingdom has the right to abide in an eternal lifestyle. Keep one thing in mind, all who are in Christ are sons of God, whether a person is male or female.

According to the Bible, in Christ there is neither male nor female.[70] While in the flesh, we may have varying roles, but when it comes to our eternal standing with God, we are all called sons. The reason the Bible uses this terminology is to give us a word picture we can understand. In the culture in which this was written, only sons received the inheritance of their fathers. Daughters married into their husband's inheritance, but rarely received a direct inheritance. The Bible makes it clear that unlike the world's traditions, whether someone was born as a male or female, all are accounted as sons in the inheritance through Christ.

Those under sin are not sons, but slaves. A slave has no inheritance. A slave did nothing but serve his or her master. Any

---

[70] Galatians 3:28

who commit sin are now in bondage to sin. To fully understand this, consider the Bible's teaching on slavery. In western culture, we tend to think of slavery according to what happened in the 1700-1800s. Slaves were captured and forced into slavery and sold as property. This is what the Bible calls 'man stealers' or kidnappers. It is condemned explicitly in scripture.[71]

When the Bible speaks of slavery, it is speaking of the legal system of the Old Testament, which was designed to protect those who go into debt and could not pay. When someone borrowed money, they entered into an agreement to pay back the money with either money or servitude. If they could not repay, they had to serve the lender as a slave until they paid the debt.

This is the picture of slavery to sin. All have sinned, and sin creates a debt to the Law. For this reason, each person is indebted to sin and it is our slave master. This is why Jesus paid the debt. When Jesus was on the cross, one of His last declarations was to cry out, "Tetelestai." Most Bibles translate this as 'it is finished', but the literal translation is 'the debt is finished' or 'the debt is paid'. Tetelestai is what was written on the bills of those who paid their debt in full. This is the only way a person can be freed from the debt of sin. Until we enter into the covenant of Christ by faith, we stand as a slave to sin. But when we become a child of God, our old man is crucified and we are set free from that debt. Look at **Romans 6:6-7**

> [6] knowing this, that our old man was crucified with *Him*, that the body of sin might be done away with, that we should no longer be slaves of sin.
> [7] For he who has died has been freed from sin.

Now that we are set free, why would we want to submit ourselves back under bondage? This is why the Bible says, "Sin wars against my mind, trying to bring me back into the captivity of sin that remains in my body."[72] Consider the words of **Romans 6:15-16**

---

[71] 1 Timothy 1:10
[72] Romans 7:23

¹⁵ What then? Shall we sin because we are not under law but under grace? Certainly not!
¹⁶ Do you not know that to whom you present yourselves slaves to obey, you are that one's slaves whom you obey, whether of sin *leading* to death, or of obedience *leading* to righteousness?

The message of scripture is that we have been set free, but that doesn't mean we can't submit to sin as our master again. Before Christ, we were indebted to sin and it was our master without our will. We had no right to be free because we were in debt. Now that we are free, sin has no right over us. Sin can only rule over the heart that submits to it. The only way a Christian can be in bondage to sin is to submit to it.

A Christian submitted to sin can be just as much in bondage as those who never knew Christ at all. The more our minds are submitted to sin, the more in bondage we become. Yet we have the right to be free. In reality we are free; however, the one who lives in sin has lost sight of their freedom and sin will rule their life.

So what is the solution to a Christian who has become enslaved to sin again? How did that person become free before being entangled? They trusted in Christ for deliverance. After coming to Christ, nothing changes. We live by faith, walk by faith, and overcome by faith. Everything in the Christian's life is by faith. Sin is not by faith; it comes by unbelief. We don't believe God's warning. We don't believe Christ can satisfy our hearts. We put our trust in sin and submit to it. We escape sin by putting our trust in Christ and submitting to righteousness.

There is nothing you can do to defeat sin, for it has already been defeated. Sin bluffs you into submission, but has no power other than what you give it. When you believe God, you will trust enough to submit to His righteousness and then you exercise your right to walk in liberty. Then you must live according to this command in **Galatians 5:1**
> Stand fast therefore in the liberty by which Christ has made us free, and do not be entangled again with a yoke of bondage.

According to the Bible, what must we do to obtain liberty? Nothing. Stand firmly in the liberty you have already been given, and don't allow yourself to be entangled by the deception of sin. It beckons, but you can stand fast in your freedom. It extends the yoke of bondage, but you don't have to receive it. The yoke of bondage is wrapped in many false promises and decorations, but it's still bondage.

Walk in liberty. Enjoy freedom. Look expectantly to Christ for satisfaction and you will find it. Entanglement never satisfies, but living as a child of the Lord and as an inheritor of the kingdom does!

Religious Bondage

There is a subtle form of bondage that entraps many sincere Christians. Legalistic religion masquerades as godliness, but there is a clear way to unmask its true source. The Bible makes it clear that whatever is not of faith is sin.[73] Not only that, but we've already examined the Bible's instruction that without faith it is impossible to please God.

Everything in God's Kingdom is by faith. Everything in the Christian life is by faith. When the Bible says faith, it is always faith in Him. We trust in what God has promised. We trust in what God has done. We trust in God's love. Name anything in the Christian life and it is always about believing God and trusting in Him. But legalism is not so.

Legalism doesn't trust God, so it implements rules. It teaches that God's righteousness given to us through Christ is not sufficient, so we have to do our part to complete the work. Many under legalism declare that Christ's is sufficient with their lips, but if people believe this then they wouldn't turn to human effort instead of receiving of Christ by faith. At the heart of legalism is a distrust in the word of God.

---

[73] Romans 14:23

Churches don't trust in God's promise that He transforms us as we learn to walk by faith. Because we don't believe the Holy Spirit has the power to change the lives of our members, churches make rules so that people are stripped from liberty and 'protected' from sin by external restraints. "Don't do these things and you will be right with God," is the message. "Do these things and God will be pleased with your life," is the list of do's. Then lists are taught. The list grows into denominationalism. Churches become rigid in their demands and hostile to anyone who doesn't conform to their regulations. The Bible addresses this very thing in **Galatians 2:4-5**

> ⁴ And *this occurred* because of false brethren secretly brought in (who came in by stealth to spy out our liberty which we have in Christ Jesus, that they might bring us into bondage),
> ⁵ to whom we did not yield submission even for an hour, that the truth of the gospel might continue with you.

People were coming into Gentile churches and saying, "Sure grace forgives you of sin, but now you must keep these rules in order to stay right with God." In some cases, the rules were implemented to complete the work of salvation. For the Galatian church, circumcision was the focus. For the modern church the focus is on numerous other things. Each denomination has its own form of circumcision.

Notice the result of the Christ-plus rules. These were called false brethren because they were not focused on Christ, but instead were trying to take people out of liberty and put them under the bondage of religion. To escape the bondage of sin only to erect bars of religion is not liberty.

It is not the churches right to take on the role of the Holy Spirit and become the conscience of its members. And it never works. Legalism does not free members from sin; it merely substitutes the sin of pleasure with the sin of self-righteousness.

Legalism is just as much a source of bondage as sin. Yes, legalism is sin because it is not by faith. It takes our trust away from God and His power, and places our trust in man's power to keep himself pure. Or it places our trust in human leadership instead of Christ. Or it places our trust in a system of religion as the power to do the work God has reserved for Himself alone.

Many who live by legalism deny that they are legalists. Perhaps we should clarify what legalism is. Legalism is to attempt to make yourself right, do good works, or keep yourself in God's will by human effort. It is to focus on any law other than the law of faith.[74] Those who try to become right with God by the Ten Commandments or Old Testament Law are legalists, but this is not the only legalism.

The Law became sin to those who tried to make themselves righteous by trusting in their efforts; in the same way, any system of religion that trusts in our deeds instead of trusting in Christ is a new form of the law. The gospel teaches that Jesus completed the work of God and fulfilled the law, and by faith we receive His work to our account. The Christian life is about trusting and receiving from Christ. Anything that does not receive righteousness from Christ is a form of legalism, for it trusts in human effort instead of trusting in Christ.

The evidence of this truth is all around us, and it's sprinkled throughout history. The more legalistic the church is, the more oppressed the members are and the more love is lost. If someone isn't obeying out of the overflow of love given to us *from* God and the overflow of love *for* God, obedience means nothing.

Consider God's word to the church at Ephesus in Revelation 2. They labored, did good works, hated evil, tested the teachings of those claiming to be of God and identified them as liars, had perseverance, and did all this for Jesus' name, but look at what Jesus said to this church in **Revelation 2:4-5**

> [4] "Nevertheless I have *this* against you, that you have left your first love.
> [5] "Remember therefore from where you have fallen; repent and do the first works, or else I will come to you quickly and remove your lampstand from its place-- unless you repent.

This message is to the church who has lost focus. This is not a threat against the individual Christian who struggles. Despite all

---

[74] Romans 3:27

the church's good works, because they left the love of God behind, they received the warning that God would remove them from their place in His work. God warned that they had to repent (or turn) from their works focused mindset and return to the love of God.

God praised them for their works, but outside of the love of God, the works could not make them right with God.

How many legalistic churches have shot their wounded instead of bearing them up in love. Certainly there will be people who don't respond to the love of God, but we must allow them to depart if they so choose. To put the people under fear in order to force behavior misses the entire truth of Christ. We should not obey out of a fear of God's wrath, but rather because we recognize the greatness of His love.

Many people are cast out of churches because they asked the wrong question, or because they struggled to overcome the flesh. Yet even the members in good standing have their own secret questions and hide their own struggles. Instead of caring for one another, alleviating doubts with truth, and bearing up those who are weak, legalism uses fear to cause people to hide their struggles out of fear of rejection.

Once a man told me he struggled with pornography. He went to his church for help and was publicly rebuked before the congregation. When they shamed him for seeking help, they claimed to be protecting the members from temptation. In reality, they were telling the congregation, "If you have a struggle, you better hide it. Don't look for help in this place."

Yet the Bible teaches the opposite. Bear the infirmities of the weak. Consider yourself, for you also can be tempted. Look to Christ and be changed.

When the Christian struggles with sin, the message of the gospel is, "Trust in Christ, for this is the victory that overcomes the world, our faith." Our responsibility as both teachers and brethren is to help one another find comfort in the love of God, and remind each other that even after failure, we have victory in Christ.

This is why James 5:16 tells us to confess our trespasses to one another. This doesn't mean we are required to broadcast every sin before the congregation, but that we share how we are overcoming through faith, in spite of our own failures. When our brother sins, we have the opportunity to say, "I've been there. God didn't reject me, but as I learned to trust in God's love, God subdued this sin and it no longer controls me." Or to testify that we still struggle with these things, but God pulls us out of the mire and places us back onto the path of righteousness.

If I struggle with the same sin that is defeating you, wouldn't you be encouraged to persevere when I testify how I'm growing closer to God, and His love is working to defeat this area of weakness in my life?

Those who are forced to conform to a standard by human effort are also forced to hide their internal battles. Their lives aren't changed. They only learn how to present a public persona of holiness and then judge those whose religious mask slip off. However, those who are of faith discover that God isn't seething with anger, but instead offers to exchange their weakness for His love. Along with this is the promise that it isn't their responsibility to change themselves, but instead we are called to trust in Him and allow the Holy Spirit to transform us into His image.

Legalism gives the pretense of a changed life that is volatile and dependent upon man's ability to hold everything together. True Christianity is God's call to trust in His love, grace, and mercy – even when we fall short. As we learn to receive of God, sin finds no place and is rooted out of our lives. Which version of the gospel do you think will have lasting change? Which gives liberty, and which is bondage? If religion creates bondage, it isn't of God, but is still rooted in the slavery of sin.

Inheritance

One of the greatest consequences to sin in the Christian life is trading in our eternal inheritance for the things of this passing life. Consider the words of **Hebrews 12:14-17**

> [14] Pursue peace with all *people*, and holiness, without which no one will see the Lord:

¹⁵ looking carefully lest anyone fall short of the grace of God; lest any root of bitterness springing up cause trouble, and by this many become defiled;
¹⁶ lest there *be* any fornicator or profane person like Esau, who for one morsel of food sold his birthright.
¹⁷ For you know that afterward, when he wanted to inherit the blessing, he was rejected, for he found no place for repentance, though he sought it diligently with tears.

While sexual immorality is specifically mentioned, it is not the only thing mentioned. Sexual temptation is one of the greatest tools of the enemy to lure the Christian into a moment-of-gratification mindset. Yet it isn't only sexual temptation that robs us. The Bible says 'or profane person'. 'Profane' is translated from the Greek word 'bebelos', which means: common, unhallowed, or public place.

Profane is something that has no value. It's also used to refer to the common place people trod over. It's the pathways everyone walks over on the road to nowhere in particular.

Let's look at the example of Esau. Esau was the firstborn son of Isaac. He was the grandson of Abraham. The firstborn son had great things to inherit. He received a double portion of his father's possessions. He was to be the leader of the next generation. The firstborn also carried the family blessing. God blessed Abraham and promised that he would be the lineage that would one day lead to Christ. The firstborn received that spiritual birthright and carried it into the next generation.

The Bible says that Esau cared nothing for his birthright. One day he came in from a hard day and was famished. Jacob was cooking himself a stew, and Esau begged for it. Jacob said, "I'll give you this stew if you will give me your birthright." Esau was only looking at the cravings of his flesh, and his spiritual promise had little value in comparison to his desire, so he sold his spiritual inheritance to Jacob for a moment of satisfaction.

When Esau showed despite to his birthright, the Lord rejected him. Jacob's mother then got a great idea. When Isaac was on his deathbed, she disguised Jacob with his brother's clothing, and he persuaded his blind father to bless him with the full inheritance of the family. When Esau returned to get the blessing, he found it had already been given to Jacob. Because the blessing was given as a declaration of God's blessing, it couldn't be changed. Esau wept bitterly, but no amount of weeping could obtain the blessing that was lost.

This is a life-example for the Christian. While people are focused on the possessions, places of honor, status, and other external ideas of blessings, they don't realize that the blessing of Christ comes through our spiritual birthright. If we forfeit who we are as a child of God in order to pursue the world, we can't expect to inherit the blessing of God's promises.

Seek first the kingdom of God and His righteousness, and then all these things will be added to you.[75] Consider the promise of **Psalm 36:7-8**

> [7] How precious *is* Your lovingkindness, O God! Therefore the children of men put their trust under the shadow of Your wings.
> [8] They are abundantly satisfied with the fullness of Your house, And You give them drink from the river of Your pleasures.

Where does this promise begin? We first believe that God is rich in favor toward us; therefore we trust in Him. He is our provider, and the one who satisfies fully. God doesn't just promise satisfaction, but to be abundantly satisfied. Those who truly understand what it means to trust completely in God, will overflow with God's pleasures. And the Bible says that God's pleasures add no sorrows.[76] This is not something you can say about finding pleasure in the world.

The only reason Christians lack satisfaction is because they have not learned what it means to trust under the shadow of God's wings. This is a word picture of a protective mother bird. Her chicks look to her alone for both protection and their every need of life. The average Christian looks to God when they feel desperation, but the call is to trust for everything. Unless we are trusting fully in His grace, we will miss much of the satisfaction that is a normal part of walking by faith.

---

[75] Matthew 6:33
[76] Proverbs 10:22

People grapple for the things of life because they feel satisfaction is dependent upon getting their fair share. We look to people for acceptance and approval. We look to the world for pleasures and possessions. We look to ourselves for self-worth and confidence. Then we get frustrated when people and things fail us. Yet no one and no thing is designed to meet your needs.

Nothing outside of faith can have lasting satisfaction. But when we receive everything by faith and people fall short, we don't become bitter, for God is our focus. When pleasures lack, God is our satisfaction. When things escape our grasp, we trust in the Lord to meet our every need. It's only when we step out from under God's wings to pursue people, pleasures, and things that we feel deprived. Unfortunately, most of us live in this state because we have not learned what it means to walk by faith.

The Christian who learns the trustworthiness of God's loving kindness obtains what everyone is seeking after. Since our provision is received from the hand of the Lord, God becomes our satisfaction instead of an object or person. He indeed gives pleasures to His children, but the pleasure never becomes the focus. When gratifying our desires is the focus, we will make foolish decisions because desire blinds us to the consequences. Once we gratify our longing through our own efforts, emptiness always follows. The reason is because the thing we put our focus on has now been obtained and has passed away. We then have no focus, but must find another desire to pursue.

This is why the world and worldly Christians spend their entire lives pursuing things and pleasures, but the quest for fulfillment never satisfies. A moment of gratification will temporarily quench the desire, but it can never satisfy, for the heart cannot satisfy itself. Yet the one who seeks God is always satisfied. When God gives pleasure, we enjoy His kindness, but our focus is never lost. We are abundantly satisfied from the river of His pleasures, but our trust is in Him instead of in pleasures or things.

The Bible is warning the Christian to not allow profane or worthless things to draw them away from grace. The heart focused on grace is the heart that trusts in God for everything. When we are certain of His loving kindness, we will trust under His wings knowing that no good thing will He withhold from those who walk with Him.[77]

Esau was not rejected as part of his family. Nor was he disavowed from all inheritance. However, he forfeited the greater blessing for a moment of profane pleasure. The Bible warns us not to forfeit God's goodness for the world that is failing and passing away. This is also reiterated in **Revelation 3:11-12**

> [11] "Behold, I am coming quickly! Hold fast what you have, that no one may take your crown.
> [12] "He who overcomes, I will make him a pillar in the temple of My God, and he shall go out no more. And I will write on him the name of My God and the name of the city of My God, the New Jerusalem, which comes down out of heaven from My God. And *I will write on him* My new name.

If you read chapters 2 and 3 of Revelation, seven times will you see the words, "To him who overcomes, I will give..." The greatest promises are to those who overcome. Any who are in Christ will find salvation, but only those who overcome will receive the full inheritance.

And here is the good news. How do we overcome? Jesus said, "Be of good cheer, for I have overcome the world."[78] 1 John 4:4 tells us that God's children overcome because He who is in us is greater than he who is in the world. In other words, you have already overcome, if you hold fast to Christ. The problem is that we are lured into the world where defeat lives. Then we spend so much of our lives trying to win victories through a defeated lifestyle. In the world you cannot find victory. In Christ, you already have victory and are already an overcomer. Look at **1 John 5:4**

> For whatever is born of God overcomes the world. And this is the victory that has overcome the world-- our faith.

---

[77] Psalm 84:11
[78] John 16:33

Do you believe God? Then walk as an overcomer. It is not you who overcomes anything. It is Christ in you that has already overcome. All you must do is trust fully in His work and not allow anyone to take your crown.

Isn't this message an interesting concept? You've probably heard that you must earn your crown. We hear people teach that we get crowns by doing the right kinds of works. Yet according to the Bible, you already have the crown given to you, and you're goal is to not allow anyone to take it. You see, the gifts of God are just that. You don't earn your crown, you have been crowned through Christ. His work has already given you EVERYTHING that pertains to life and godliness through Christ. Temptation is the enemy's tool to rob you of what you have been given.

How does someone take your crown? You are invited to trade your crown for greed. Or the lusts of the world. Or the pride of life. When you are provoked into anger, it's actually spiritual warfare, where Satan is attempting to draw you out of your walk of faith so you take hold of the flesh to handle life by your own power.

Temptation is the call to let go of the power of God, where victory is guaranteed, and to take the horns of the flesh, where victory is an impossibility. Even if we win something through the flesh, it's still a loss of what was given through the Spirit. All temptation attempts to draw you into the flesh where only this world can be served and inherited.

Even so, don't fear. Every person has fallen to temptation. The Bible says that a wise man will fall, but get up again. It isn't those who stumble who lose their crown. It is those who abandon the way of faith to fulfill life through the flesh who lose the crown.

The wonderful news of God's mercies is that when we fail, we don't grovel in failure. We don't stay in the flesh and try to fix it. When we fail, we recognize we have stopped walking by faith and are now acting out in the flesh. The answer is to refocus on the truth of God's favor.

We must look back to the truth that Christ already dealt with sin. We put our trust in the forgiveness He has already given us, and we trust in His strength to overcome our weaknesses through the power of God placed within us. Faith says, "I failed when I took control. I surrender myself to Your grace again, and I believe in your promise – greater is Christ within me than all that is in the world." Then walk confidently in faith.

The person who forfeits the promises of God is not the one who blows it. It is the one who is persuaded to live this life by their own power. They try to gratify themselves by grappling for temptation. They trust in the promise of temptation and don't believe God is truly the giver of all good. They abandon trust in God and seek to avenge their own feelings and wrongs by human effort. Whether that be a bitter spirit, passive aggressive behavior, or trying to return wrongs, we are choosing the flesh if we become the one who must right the wrong, or the one who wallows in the wrongs done to us.

The person who doesn't believe in the completed work of Christ is also forfeiting their crown. That person is trusting in their own works and their own righteousness in order to earn God's favor. God has declared that His favor cannot be bought with money or works. It can only be received through Christ. The one who trusts in themselves cannot walk by faith in the victory of Christ.

What about works?

The natural question that arises from this discussion is, "Does this mean we do nothing?" This question was addressed in the chapter on works, but let's add another few nuggets of truth into the discussion. Let's look at **1 Corinthians 3:11-15**

> [11] For no other foundation can anyone lay than that which is laid, which is Jesus Christ.
>
> [12] Now if anyone builds on this foundation *with* gold, silver, precious stones, wood, hay, straw,
>
> [13] each one's work will become clear; for the Day will declare it, because it will be revealed by fire; and the fire will test each one's work, of what sort it is.
>
> [14] If anyone's work which he has built on *it* endures, he will receive a reward.

> [15] If anyone's work is burned, he will suffer loss; but he himself will be saved, yet so as through fire.

What is the focus of these works? Everything is built upon the foundation of Jesus Christ. Don't miss the most important part of this truth. This is the life built upon Jesus. The natural result is good fruit. When Jesus discussed the necessity for abiding in Him, He said, "He who abides in Me and I in him, bears much fruit, for without me you can do nothing."

Those who have Christ must focus their life on abiding in Him. It is a life walk of faith. If you are abiding in Christ, you will bear fruit. It's a guarantee, for a life founded upon Christ that also abides in Christ can do no other. Our works are the outflow of the Holy Spirit within us as we focus on walking in fellowship with God. Good works are the natural result of the love of God in our hearts. Any who do not abide will not be focused on Christ and will be distracted by both temptation to sin, and the temptation to produce their own fruit outside of Christ.

The distracted person may still want to do good works, but all they can produce is wood, hay, and straw. These are the works of man, done by human effort, and presented to God as good. Yet the Bible makes it clear that anything born of the flesh is flesh and not acceptable to God.[79]

Notice what the above passage states. Their works will be burned and they will suffer loss, but the person born of Christ will remain even if their works do not. The eternal life we have been given is by God and cannot be harmed by the fire of judgment. It will pass into eternity unharmed, but all the works of the flesh it carried will be burned away, for nothing of the flesh can pass over.

That which is built upon Christ will endure, for nothing can be laid on that foundation other than that which is of Christ. Our lives are built on an eternal foundation, and as we receive from God, we take what He gives and build it into our foundation. And the amazing part is this – God rewards us for receiving from Him.

---

[79] John 3:6

He provides, and then He rewards us for trusting in His provision and building our lives upon faith in Him.

Hopefully you see that the consequences of choosing sin is the loss of what God was providing. When we turn to sin, we are pushing aside the work of God. We can't build with both the flesh and the Spirit. Those who trust in the flesh, build a foundation that will be a complete loss. Those who live by faith are building on a foundation that cannot fail. And then we are rewarded for receiving the work of God into our lives. It's all about grace – the gift of Christ's completed work.

Chastisement

What does a parent do when they see their children acting in a way that will cause harm? They intervene. What parent would allow their toddler to play in the road? Or play with knives? Or stick things in power outlets?

As parents, we train our children to behave for their good. While it's only natural that we act in selfish ways as parents, we are still capable of foreseeing consequences and forcing behavior in our kids to avoid those consequences. Sometimes the consequence is an immediate danger. We spring into action to protect their safety. We might see an oncoming car and snatch the child out of the road. Or slap their hand off the power outlet.

From the child's perspective, they feel violated. They have no comprehension of the danger. They only know that they were snatched away from what looked good to their eyes. Consider the attitudes of teens. Whether it was our teen years, or our kids, teenagers believe something is good, but parents clearly see the end results. We have life experience and a perspective they have no view of. We've seen our friends suffer terrible consequences. We've witnessed or even have experienced the end of the road our teens want to travel. We stand in the way because we care, but they can only see our interference in their lives.

How much more true is this with the Lord? The One who created all things, laid the timeline of history, and knows the end result of everything, fully understands where we are going and what is down each path we consider. God will snatch you out of danger that you cannot see. He will block you from paths that look good to you. And you will lash out at Him as if He is cruel and uncaring. Yet, like a good parent, He will stand firm regardless of our feelings.

And this is the role of chastisement. It is not punishment; it is correction. It is intended to correct the attitudes that place selfishness as the goal of life. Or the quest for desires that are entrapments. Chastisement is not God's goal. The goal is perfect fellowship. Correction only serves to turn us away from the pathways of destruction, and only last until we are on the right way. As Proverbs states, there is a way that seems right to us, but the end is the way of destruction.[80] Correction leads us away from that path. Let's take a moment to dig into the Bible's discussion of chastisement in **Hebrews 12:5-8**

> [5] And you have forgotten the exhortation which speaks to you as to sons: "My son, do not despise the chastening of the LORD, Nor be discouraged when you are rebuked by Him;
> [6] For whom the LORD loves He chastens, And scourges every son whom He receives."
> [7] If you endure chastening, God deals with you as with sons; for what son is there whom a father does not chasten?
> [8] But if you are without chastening, of which all have become partakers, then you are illegitimate and not sons.
> ...
> [11] Now no chastening seems to be joyful for the present, but painful; nevertheless, afterward it yields the peaceable fruit of righteousness to those who have been trained by it.

What is the ultimate goal of chastisement? It is to produce peace and righteousness and to train us to receive this fruit. I wanted to review this passage since there are both nuggets of truth to glean, and things that should be clarified. Before digging out the nuggets, let's address a misconception caused by the way this is translated. In this passage, the writer of Hebrews is quoting from **Proverbs 3:11-12**

---

[80] Proverbs 14:12, Proverbs 16:25

> [11] My son, do not despise the chastening of the LORD, Nor detest His correction;
> [12] For whom the LORD loves He corrects, Just as a father the son *in whom* he delights.

Do you notice anything different about the wording? Hebrews mentions scourging, but Proverbs only mentions the father being delighted in his child.

The word scourge and scourging is mentioned 24 times in the Bible. In every instance, it is either the punishment of the wicked, or it is the righteous being punished by the wicked. Not once is it given in any context other than punishment. There is only one time where God is credited with scourging (or punishing) the righteous. It is found in **Isaiah 53:3-6**

> [3] He is despised and rejected by men, A Man of sorrows and acquainted with grief. And we hid, as it were, *our* faces from Him; He was despised, and we did not esteem Him.
> [4] Surely He has borne our griefs And carried our sorrows; Yet we esteemed Him stricken, Smitten by God, and afflicted.
> [5] But He *was* wounded for our transgressions, *He was* bruised for our iniquities; The chastisement for our peace *was* upon Him, And by His stripes we are healed.
> [6] All we like sheep have gone astray; We have turned, every one, to his own way; And the LORD has laid on Him the iniquity of us all.

By His stripes we are healed. The stripes laid on Christ's back were by the scourging of the Roman soldiers (See Matthew 27:26). The blows of the whip were delivered through the soldiers who beat Him, but according to God's declaration in Isaiah, it was actually God punishing our sin through Christ. With scourging, there is always condemnation. Jesus was scourged, mocked, and condemned. And God laid the iniquities of us all on Him (Christ). By His stripes we are healed. We are not scourged with Christ. We are delivered from scourging through Christ.

Scourging is when a condemned man is declared worthy of stripes. The punisher would take the scourge, which is a whip, and lay severe stripes across the back of the guilty. The average man could endure forty stripes before death became a real possibility.

This is why the Jews implemented a law where 39 stripes was the limit.

The Romans took scourging to a new level. They began placing bits of rock or metal on the end of the whips. Unlike the Jews, their goal was death. When the Romans scourged a condemned man, it was part of a death penalty. This is why Jesus was unable to carry the cross all the way up the hill at His crucifixion. His beating was so marring that a bystander had to be summons to help Him carry the cross.[81]

Do you see a problem between the concept of scourging the Christian and what God has declared in Isaiah 53 and the New Testament gospel? Our punishment was laid on Christ. He took the stripes of scourging on our behalf. In Christ, there is now no condemnation.[82] Scourging is the punishment of the condemned, not the correction of those called justified children of God.

In the context of correction in the above passage in Hebrews, we are told this is for the child God is receiving – not the person rejected for condemnation. Godly chastisement is for those in which the Father is delighted. Stop for a moment to think on this truth. It is the son in whom God is delighted. It is for the child God is receiving as His own. Correction is because God is delighted in you and He rejoices in your way.[83]

It isn't punishment, but correction. It isn't for those condemned for their sins, but for those received as their father's delight. Because your Heavenly Father is delighted in you and has *already* received you, He corrects your paths so you can receive every benefit of His kingdom. That is the goal of correction.

Is that a selfish gospel? Far from it. Who is more self-focused? Those who are offered a gift from their father, but snub the gesture of love and turn away? Or the one who receives it with gratitude?

Our attitude toward correction should be the same as our attitude toward God's gifts – gratitude and expectation of good. A

---

[81] Matthew 27:32, Mark 15:21, Luke 23:26
[82] Romans 8:1
[83] Psalm 37:23

child of God who has learned to trust in Him will look at each situation in life with expectancy. We are anticipating God's good, and trusting in correction, knowing that it will produce the fruit of peace as we open our eyes to His leading hand.

Which child is loved the most, the one who heeds correction, or the one who is stubborn and forces the more severe correction? Okay, that was a trick question. Both are equally loved. But which will experience that love the most? Obviously, the one who turns at God's rebuke will experience God's favor the most. God's favor is laid out before each of us, but to experience it, we must be walking on the path of God's will – for all favor is in His presence.

God loves the Christian who submits to correction and looks expectantly for God's favor in everything. They trust God, and because they walk by faith, they experience the fullness of God's favor. The more they learn to walk by faith, the more they experience the favor that has been set before them.

God also loves the stubborn Christian – those who will not submit. The stubborn life is focused on selfishness, living for the flesh, and believes that their understanding is more trustworthy than God's word and leading hand. This is the person who grieves the Spirit.[84] Just as a parent is grieved when a child is determined to follow mischief and their own ways, God is grieved when His children kick against correction and are determined to invest their lives in a world destined for destruction. His love doesn't fail, but the stubborn Christian doesn't experience that love. His favor is laid before them, but they can't walk in that favor because they are filling their lives with what is contrary to faith.

Many Christians suffer needlessly because they fight against correction instead of trusting in the One correcting them. Pride causes them to act out in bitterness against God or against others. We have a tendency to cling to what is destroying us, and we feel the chastisement of God and the weight of our attitudes. Yet we won't give in. I don't understand why this is true, but it's something we all struggle with to varying degrees. Yet when we

---

[84] Ephesians 4:30

let go of what God is purging, we discover peace and then wonder why we were so stubborn. But the next time we'll wrestle with self-will again.

The solution is to stop looking at anything but our Savior. When you believe He is good and trust Him completely, then you can adopt an attitude of gratitude even when you don't understand the trials of life.

Also understand that not every trial of life is God's chastisement. We live in a fallen world. Pain is a part of life. We have the privilege of allowing Him to carry our pain and ourselves. Sometimes pain is the result of consequences. Sometimes pain is part of God's correction. Sometimes pain is the reality of a fallen world that reminds us that we have a greater hope awaiting.

Life lived with the focus on the 70-year perspective won't seem fair. It's not fair that someone who works less got promoted over me. It's not fair that I was wronged. It's not fair that the wicked prosper. However, when I look at life through eternal eyes in the Spirit, everything changes. Great is my hope, and losing something in this life isn't worthy of even being compared to the hope God reveals.[85] God gives us far above what we deserve, so what can be lost that we should mourn over in this life?

And this is the purpose of correction. It is to take our eyes off what is dying in the 70-year life, and walk in new life which promises a full inheritance. In that day, all pain will be forgotten. Not forgotten from memory, but replaced with what was once hoped for but now has become sight.

Discussion Questions:

When we teach or are taught to look for sin in our lives, what becomes our focus?

Can focusing on sin produce spiritual victory?

---

[85] Romans 8:18

Does declaring our sin before God deny or affirm the victory we have been given by Christ?

Read Acts 10:9-14. How does this apply to our lives in Christ?

Read John 15:3, Hebrews 10:2, and 2 Peter 1:9. If God has declared us clean and purified, are we wrong to declare what God has cleansed to be unclean?

When we declare ourselves unclean, are we looking at the flesh, or the spirit? Which does God see when looking at us?

Who is fleshly minded, the person who willfully sins or the person who focuses on the sins already committed?

Why can the Christian not be at ease in sin?

When we feel unaccepted or cling to guilt, are we trusting in human emotions or in God's promises?

How are people set free from the bondage of sin? If a Christian falls back into sin, how are they set free?

Explain what legalism is.

Can you depend on your own efforts and still walk by faith? Explain.

Does God's love cease when we sin or blow it?

What does it mean to trust under the shadow of God's wings?

Where do good works come from?

Why will some of our works be burned and become a loss at the day of Christ?

When God chastens us, is it His wrath?

How is chastisement the evidence of God's delight in us?

Is the Christian punished for sin? Explain.

The Wayward Christian

If there is one chapter that will be controversial, this is it. Even if you don't agree with this chapter, we can still be friends. However, I believe if we allow ourselves to be honest and let the scriptures speak, we are compelled to the conclusion I'll be discussing here.

Before delving into the wayward Christian, I want to discuss something I covered in my book, Simple Faith – the covenants of God. God delivered two covenants to man in the scriptures. There are many covenants, but only two confirmed by God with God. The covenant of the Law was dependent upon man, but the covenant of the promise of Abraham was not man-dependent. The old covenant was made with Abraham and his descendants. It was a covenant of faith, but was based on entering the covenant by circumcision. Circumcision was a sign of God's covenant where a male child had the foreskin of his flesh removed as an outward testimony of entering into God's promise.

You can read where God delivered the covenant in Genesis 15. All covenants of God are confirmed as a blood oath, but never is man the one who confirms the oath. When God set Abraham aside as a chosen father of Israel, Abraham was asked to prepare the sacrifice, but Abraham was not permitted to confirm the oath. In the ancient world, when two parties entered into a binding agreement, they would slay an animal, divide it in two, and lay each half to the side. Both parties would then swear an oath and walk between the pieces. The guarantee was that if either party broke the oath, it was a death sentence, just as it had been with the animal. It was like saying, "So shall it be done to me as it was done to this animal if I should break my oath."

Abraham prepared the sacrifice, then God caused a deep sleep to fall on Abraham. He was able to see it as a vision, but Abraham was not permitted to pass through the sacrifice. The Father and Christ appear as a smoking oven and a burning torch. This is why the Bible says, "For when God made a promise to

Abraham, because He could swear by no one greater, He swore by Himself." (Hebrews 6:13).

The first covenant could only be broken by God taking upon Himself the death penalty He had sworn. This meant that Abraham could not break the covenant, nor could his descendants. It was confirmed by God in Christ and was not dependent upon man.

Four-hundred years after the covenant was confirmed, the Law was given through Moses. Even the Old Covenant was received by faith. Consider **Galatians 3:17**

> And this I say, *that* the Law, which was four hundred and thirty years later, cannot annul the covenant that was confirmed before by God in Christ, that it should make the promise of no effect.

Once again, who confirmed the Old Covenant? It was by God in Christ. Not by Abraham. Not by man's ability to measure up. The Law served to expose sin in our fallen nature so we were driven to Christ for redemption, but the nation of Israel was assured of the covenant of Abraham whether they were righteous or not. Only refusing circumcision could cut someone off from the Old Covenant.[86] People could be cut off from fellowship for other things, but they could not be cut off from the covenant of promise.

The promise was that God would lead them into the Promised Land and would establish them. Yet after the people turned from God and broke the covenant of the Law, they were judged, but the promise remained. God promised to take the remnant of Israel and establish them as a people with hope.[87]

Because the people trusted in the nations around them, many abandoned the promise and sought hope from the world. The covenant was spiritual, as indicated by the cutting away of the flesh of the foreskin, but when the people turned back to the flesh, they stepped outside of the promise.

---

[86] Genesis 17:4
[87] Jeremiah 33

In the New Covenant, we also see the confirmation by God alone. Man prepared the sacrifice of Christ, but man was not the confirmation of the promise of the eternal life in God's kingdom. The New Covenant was also confirmed by God in Christ. The Father laid the burden of sin upon the Son, and the Son sacrificed Himself upon the cross. He broke the Old Covenant[88] and paid the penalty of sin according to the Law.

Now we enter that covenant just as the Jews did. They had the symbol of the flesh cut away from the outward skin, and we have the flesh nature cut away from our hearts.[89] When someone trusts in Christ, the Spirit takes away the old sinful nature and establishes us into the promise by a new nature born through the Spirit.[90]

Since the covenant is based on the completed work of Christ, you cannot break the covenant. This means that even when you slip back into a fleshly way of thinking and act out in sin, you remain secured by the covenant of Christ. The Law failed because it was dependent upon man living in perfection. The Law is spiritual, but we are of the flesh. The flesh can never live by an eternal spiritual mindset.

Though the Law is just as much alive today as it was in the Old Testament, when God circumcises our heart, the old nature is put to death and we are given a new spiritual nature. The Law only applies to our old nature. Look at **Romans 6:7-9**

> [7] For he who has died has been freed from sin.
> [8] Now if we died with Christ, we believe that we shall also live with Him,
> [9] knowing that Christ, having been raised from the dead, dies no more. Death no longer has dominion over Him.

Romans 8:2 For the Law of the Spirit of life in Christ Jesus has made me free from the Law of sin and death.

In Christ, we are freed from the Law. Now we live in Christ – who has fulfilled the Law on our behalf. We enjoy the benefits of

---

[88] Zechariah 11:10-17
[89] Jeremiah 4:4, Romans 2:29
[90] 2 Corinthians 5:17, 1 Peter 1:23

His labors. Since Christ is God in the flesh, He was born without a sin nature; therefore, He was able to accomplish what we could not. He was born into a body of flesh, but instead of being condemned through the flesh, He condemned sin in the flesh.[91] God took the penalty of the Law that rested upon us, and placed it upon Christ and condemned it. God then took the righteousness of Christ, and placed it to our account to liberate us from the Law.[92]

This is why we can walk in absolute confidence. While our desire is being transitioned away from the cravings of the flesh and into the love of the Spirit, we are going to commit sins. Yet we cannot break the covenant that God has confirmed in Christ. You are not the guarantee of the covenant, He is. The covenant is not based on your abilities or performance, but Christ's performance.

Up to this point, nothing should seem controversial. Though few people seem to understand this truth, it is basic Christianity. Not Christian religion, but true Christianity – based on faith and trust in Christ and His completed work.

The controversy arises because as people understand what we've discussed above, other scriptures tend to confuse people. Since people naturally lock into a specific mindset, they push aside anything that doesn't fit their beliefs. However, it's important to understand the scriptures more fully, otherwise, the scriptures you avoid will be taught in ways that will cause doubt and confusion. One such passage is **1 Corinthians 11:32**

> But when we are judged, we are chastened by the Lord, that we may not be condemned with the world.

I'm going to bring in a number of passages which give us a clear teaching as to what is being discussed here. Those who don't understand the covenant of Christ will say, "This shows that you can lose your salvation when you sin." Let me state this as plainly

---

[91] Romans 8:3
[92] Isaiah 53:6, 2 Corinthians 5:21

as possible. Your sin cannot nullify the work of Christ. If you are in Christ, there is NO condemnation.

Yet this passage seems to contradict this truth. God chastises us so we are not condemned with the world? The word here is the Greek word 'katakrino' which means condemning, punishing, or damning. It's the same word used to describe those who do not believe in Christ and die in their sins. Let's bring in a few other passages. We'll start with **2 Thessalonians 2:3**

> Let no one deceive you by any means; for *that Day will not come* unless the falling away comes first, and the man of sin is revealed, the son of perdition,

In this passage, Paul is answering a concern of a church who had been taught that Jesus had already come. Just as it is today, in the first century, many spin-off religions emerged from the church. This church became deeply troubled and wrote for an answer. In Paul's answer is a nugget of truth that applies to our discussion. There must first be a falling away before the man of sin comes on the scene. This is often referred to as the antichrist by most Christians.

That phrase 'falling away' is the Greek word 'apostasia' which means to abandon the faith or to defect. As I mentioned in a previous chapter, it is the concept of renouncing one's citizenship and declaring allegiance to another.

This DOES NOT mean to fall away from our steadfastness. If drifting away from God or falling back into sin created condemnation, we would all be doomed. Nearly every Christian testimony has a story about falling away before they really begin to grow deeper in the faith. My past is sprinkled with times of falling away, repentance, trying again, promising to stand firm, and then falling away again.

It wasn't until I discovered the things I've written here that I began to find steadfastness in my spiritual walk. Complete trust in Christ's finished work is the only thing that gave me a consistent walk. Before this understanding, I was dependent upon the same flesh that couldn't keep the Law; therefore, it was certain I couldn't keep the New Covenant. It's not my job to keep the covenant, but to trust in Christ and let Him transform me into His likeness.

Falling away is not falling into sin. It is not drifting away from God. It is to defect from the faith. Yet we have a safeguard in God's chastisement. He will chastise us with His correction so that we do not return to the condemnation of the world. Look back at the above scripture and see. Why does God chastise? So we are not condemned. Since we are no longer under condemnation in Christ, what danger could there be?

The danger is not sinning, for even the greatest Christian wrestles with sin in their lives. It is God discouraging us from going down the path that draws us back into the world. Not merely the world of sin, but the point where we defect from Christ and declare ourselves independent of Him and putting our trust in another citizenship.

A good example of this is the life of Charles Templeton. He was the co-founder of Youth for Christ International in 1946. He hired Billy Graham as the first Youth for Christ president and accomplished many great things that still are bearing fruit today. He was once considered one of the greatest evangelists and even helped mentor Billy Graham.

In 1957, after several years of struggling, he declared himself to be an atheist. Many years later, he made statements such as, "I sure miss Him [Christ]," yet he continued to propagate atheism and declared his allegiance to the cause of atheism.

For nearly a decade, his life was miserable. What he attributed to the chains of unreasonable faith was actually the hand of the Lord. Yet God does not force a person to remain faithful. We can fight against chastisement and get more angry at God rather than recognizing His desire to prevent us from getting to the point of renouncing Christ and defecting from the faith.

At this point many will say, "Templeton was never truly saved." Is this the case? Consider the words of **2 Peter 2:19-21**

> [19] While they promise them liberty, they themselves are slaves of corruption; for by whom a person is overcome, by him also he is brought into bondage.
> [20] For if, after they have escaped the pollutions of the world through the

knowledge of the Lord and Savior Jesus Christ, they are again entangled in them and overcome, the latter end is worse for them than the beginning.

²¹ For it would have been better for them not to have known the way of righteousness, than having known *it*, to turn from the holy commandment delivered to them.

Let me ask a question, if we retain eternal life, can it be said, "It would have been better for them not to have known the way of righteousness?"

Now let me ask another question. Does a lost person ever escape the pollutions of the world through the knowledge of their Lord and Savior, Jesus Christ? What about this passage from **Hebrews 6:4-6**

⁴ For *it is* impossible for those who were once enlightened, and have tasted the heavenly gift, and have become partakers of the Holy Spirit,
⁵ and have tasted the good word of God and the powers of the age to come,
⁶ if they fall away, to renew them again to repentance, since they crucify again for themselves the Son of God, and put *Him* to an open shame.

If the Bible says that someone has been delivered through their *Lord and Savior Jesus Christ*, who can refute the Bible's declaration and say, "He wasn't really their Savior?" How can anyone become a partaker of the Holy Spirit without being saved? How can one be enlightened without receiving God's transforming power? The Bible always calls the unredeemed person blind, in darkness, without knowledge, and unrighteous. The Bible never says the unredeemed have escaped corruption through their Lord and Savior, Jesus Christ. The lost are never called enlightened. People who say otherwise are trying to force the Bible to conform to their beliefs instead of drawing understanding from the scriptures.

The Bible describes a type of person who received Jesus as Lord and Savior, tasted the heavenly gift, became a partaker of God's promise, enlightened, and have seen the powers of the age to come. There is only one person who has these qualities and experiences – the Christian. The world has no power of God. They don't have enlightened eyes. They don't know the way of righteousness or escape the pollution of sin. Nor can the unregenerated person ever become a partaker of the Holy Spirit.

This *is* the description of the Christian life. This is you and I because we are partakers of God's divine nature. We have escaped, tasted the goodness of God, experience the powers of the life to come, are enlightened to the truth, have the holy commandment given to us, and have received this new life in Christ. You and I are the person described here – except for the falling away.

One of the roles of chastisement is to correct our way *so we are not condemned with the world.* Let me reiterate again, this is not falling into sin. This only applies to defecting from the faith. It is the person who has been persuaded to deny Christ, renounce their citizenship, and defect back into the world. While they may be following someone's promise of liberty, they are entangling themselves back into the world.

Templeton believed he was being freed from religion. Atheism promised freedom from legalism, and he believed this false teaching over the promise of liberty in Christ. In Hebrews above, the subject being addressed is those who are being persuaded to deny Christ and return to a religion based on sacrifice and human effort.

Let's bring in one other passage. Look at **Jude 1:11-12**
[11] Woe to them! For they have gone in the way of Cain, have run greedily in the error of Balaam for profit, and perished in the rebellion of Korah.
[12] These are spots in your love feasts, while they feast with you without fear, serving *only* themselves. *They are* clouds without water, carried about by the winds; late autumn trees without fruit, twice dead, pulled up by the roots;

Let's consider a few things from this passage. First, what was the sin of Balaam? He is the infamous prophet of God. King Balak promised Balaam abundant riches if he would turn against God and curse God's people. God would not allow Balaam to prophesy falsely, so Balaam came up with another plan. He taught Balak how to make God's people sin. Balak then used the most beautiful women in his kingdom to seduce the men of Israel, and then use sexuality to draw them away from God's promise and into idolatry. Balaam chose riches over God.

Also notice the phrase 'twice dead'. How can someone be twice dead? Without Christ, we are dead spiritually.[93] Look at
Ephesians 2:4-7
> [4] But God, who is rich in mercy, because of His great love with which He loved us,
> [5] even when we were dead in trespasses, made us alive together with Christ (by grace you have been saved),
> [6] and raised *us* up together, and made *us* sit together in the heavenly *places* in Christ Jesus,
> [7] that in the ages to come He might show the exceeding riches of His grace in *His* kindness toward us in Christ Jesus.

You were dead, but Christ has made you alive. Yet the ones God declares as troubling the church are those who are not just dead once, but twice dead. Or as both Hebrews and Peter states, these are in a position where the latter end is worse than if they had never known the way of truth. The worst of the worst can find salvation. The Apostle Paul arrested Christians and took them to the courts to be tried and executed, yet he found mercy. Prostitutes, thieves, liars, and any level of immorality can have mercy. But what hope is there for someone such as Templeton, who renounces their Lord and defects back to the world.

They have tasted Christ, but then are lured by the promise of freedom in the flesh so they can serve the flesh. While they were promise liberty, they are entangled, overcome, and the latter end is worse than the beginning, just as the Bible states.

Is this a controversial teaching? It indeed goes against the beliefs of the church, but it's mentioned in five books in the New Testament. To ignore it has two dangers. First, it blinds us to the chastisement of the Lord as He leads us away from the deception of defecting. Second, false teachers will use these passages to persuade Christians that salvation is dependent upon their ability to measure up to God's law. Then people become dependent

---

[93] Colossians 2:13,

upon their failing efforts and lose trust in Christ's completed work.

The truth is, these passages are teaching the opposite. Legalism puts us on that path, for any human effort is a denial of Christ. What was the burden of Charles Templeton? He couldn't bear the burden of living out his faith. He grew weary from having to measure up with works. He grew weary of trying to make himself believe. Every complaint he expressed was based on the spiritual exhaustion that resulted from human effort. He grew tired of bearing a burden he was never intended to carry. In the end, he trusted in his own ability to make himself believe, but grew tired of what he called pretending. The next work he produced was the book, 'Farewell to God.' It's the testimony of why he defected from the faith.

According to scripture, events in the last days will persuade many to defect from the faith. This is because the faith of the church is grounded in something other than faith in Christ. Human faith is dependent upon ourselves, but true faith is that which is received from God. It is God's revelation to us.

If God is revealing powerful truths to us, and we are experiencing His life-changing power, how can we do anything but trust? Human faith doesn't experience this power, but is dependent upon your own strength. If God's power is theoretical and not something you are experiencing, it's not a long distance into doubt and disbelief.

To be a legalist does not equate to defecting from Christ, but it does point us into a direction where the completed work of Christ is denied. God will correct you, and sometimes that correction is the burden of failed legalistic efforts. In Templeton's case, he grew more frustrated and began to listen to atheists claiming that Christ was the burden.

Those who recognize God's hand will begin to discard legalism and begin to unload their burden onto Christ where it belongs. Only then can they fully receive the gift of His work given to them. The burden has already been fulfilled and we are called to rest as we trust fully upon His grace.[94]

For we who trust in Christ's completed work, these passages are our encouragement. Even when we drift off course, God is correcting and leading us toward the way of rest and promise. If faith is a burden, then you are not resting in Christ. If works are a burden, then you are not walking in the works God prepared for you to walk in.[95] Religion is a burden, but Christ is not. He bore the burden and only asks us to walk with Him. We are yoked to the one who is carrying the weight. And sometimes He must carry us. You are never called to carry God's burden.

Do not fear that you have lost salvation. Do not fear that these passages are meant to condemn you. Each of these passages rests on one truth – trust fully in Christ and cease from your own efforts. When you fall, God is not condemning you. God has already restored you. Receive His favor with thanksgiving and rejoice in the truth that your relationship is not dependent upon you, but was sealed by God in Christ.

None of those who fall away do so because they trusted in Christ. It is always trusting in the flesh that leads us astray. Whether we are trusting in an organization and rejecting Christ, or trusting in our own works instead of Christ, it's still human effort displacing the glory of Christ. Rest in **Romans 10:11**
> For the Scripture says, "Whoever believes on Him will not be put to shame."

This is your hope and firm assurance. Never turn from this and you will never need to be concerned with the above passages. Rest in Christ.

---

[94] 1 Peter 1:13
[95] Ephesians 2:10

Discussion Questions:

Why did God not allow Abraham to confirm the Old Covenant?

Why does God not allow our efforts to be the guarantee of the New Covenant?

What does it mean when the Bible says, you are the righteousness of God in Him? Does our righteous acts improve our standing with God?

If the Bible says that someone has received Jesus as their Lord and Savior, is it saying that person is a Christian?

Can the lost person partake of the Holy Spirit? Can they experience the power of God and the life to come?

Does falling into sin take away our salvation?

What does it mean to defect from faith in Christ?

Why do people grow weary in the faith?

Read Matthew 11:28-30. Is this how most Christians operate?

If faith is a burden, is Christ the focus?

Do you think God is calling you to carry the burden of labor for Him?

Escaping the Law

When the promise of the completed work of Christ is taught, there are always one of two reactions among Christians. One is rejoicing because we can now enjoy perfect fellowship without having to carry the burden of measuring up to a standard that is humanly impossible. The other choice is the 'but' crowd. But what about the Law? But what about works.

Works have been addressed in this book, but due to the objections I've heard, addressing this more fully is necessary. Those who focus on the Law do so because they have not come to the end of themselves. They still believe they find acceptance by measuring up to God's standard by personal effort, even though the apostles of Christ said, "Why do you test God by putting a yoke on the neck of the disciples which neither our fathers nor we were able to bear?"[96]

I recently received a twenty-four page rebuttal to living by grace. The man told me it was coming, and I predicted it would be focused on the Old Testament as proof text for the Law. As predicted, it was all about the Torah. The Torah is the first five books of the Old Testament where the Law was given to Israel. While this man acknowledged Christ as the payment for our sins, he also claimed that we are given the Holy Spirit to empower us to keep the Law of the Old Testament.

This man quoted several passages where Jesus said things like, "Though heaven and earth shall pass away, not one jot or tittle will pass from the Law until all is fulfilled." To that, I'll let the Bible speak. **Romans 10:4**

> For Christ *is* the end of the Law for righteousness to everyone who believes.

Add to this Romans 8:3-4
> ³ For what the Law could not do in that it was weak through the flesh, God *did* by sending His own Son in the likeness of sinful flesh, on account

---

[96] Acts 15:10

> of sin: He condemned sin in the flesh,
> ⁴ that the righteous requirement of the Law might be fulfilled in us who do not walk according to the flesh but according to the Spirit.

Did you catch the message of verse four above? The Law *has* been fulfilled to all who are in Christ. All has been fulfilled in the life of the Christian, for we are no longer in the flesh, but are in the Spirit. There is one point in the rebuttal I completely agree with, "The Law is just as relevant today as it was in Moses' day." This is true, but only for those who are not in Christ. Any who are in the flesh ARE still under the Law, for ONLY he who has died has been set free from both the Law and the sin imputed through the Law.[97] Those who are under the Law are still in debt, for the Law does not make anyone righteous – it only reveals sin.

In every culture this is evident. Even civil law does not reward obedience. Nor does it judge based on a scale of good and bad. A million good deeds does not excuse someone who has broken the Law. Someone standing before a judge can present as many good deeds as they want, but none of the deeds can make them innocent of the law they have broken.

The Lawbreaker could say, "I fed the poor, gave to charity, helped old ladies across the street, went to church, read my Bible, prayed, and did many good deeds. I've done a lot more good things and only this one bad thing." Would this testimony move a judge? No. None of these things hold any weight.

The judge would say, "You broke the Law. According to the Law, this is your penalty. Guilty." Then the sentence would be given. The Law does not reward good behavior – it only penalizes violations of the Law. The Law does not take all the areas where the Law was kept into account. It only focuses on the breaking of the Law. Why would anyone want to live under this weight of the Law?

The Law of God is no different. Look at **Romans 3:19-20**

> ¹⁹ Now we know that whatever the Law says, it says to those who are under the Law, that every mouth may be stopped, and all the world may become guilty before God.

---

[97] Romans 6:7 and Romans 7:6

[20] Therefore by the deeds of the Law no flesh will be justified in His sight, for by the Law *is* the knowledge of sin.

Where is the merit for keeping the Law? It's not there because that isn't the purpose of the Law. According to the Bible, the Law is spiritual, but we are carnal, or of the flesh. The flesh can never enter the spiritual world; therefore, the flesh can never fulfill the Law. The Law is perfect because it is a reflection of God, but the Law is weak in that in order to be fulfilled, it is dependent on the weakness of human flesh.

Reread Romans 8:3-4 above. Is the Law weak? No. But fulfilling the Law is impossible because it depends on something that is weak – our flesh. Our flesh is corrupted by a sinful nature and therefore can never fulfill the Law. We are the weakness of the Law because we cannot rise to the level of perfection demanded by the Law.

One objection I received was that I said the Law produces sin. Actually, I didn't say it was the Law creating the sin. It arouses the flesh which produces sin. This was quoted from **Romans 7:5**
> For when we were in the flesh, the sinful passions which were aroused by the Law were at work in our members to bear fruit to death.

The Law condemns, and it arouses the flesh. The Law reveals our sin by exposing it. When the word of God is allowed to shine into man's nature, everything that is contrary to God is made manifest (or revealed). The Law exposes our failures – it does not reveal our goodness.

There are only two choices for those who desire to follow God. They must either be under the Law, or under the promise. The Law produces guilt, but the promise gives us God's gift of grace. There is no mixture, though people often try to mix these two. According to the Bible, if we put ourselves under the Law, we are debtors to do the whole law. Consider these two passages:
> **Galatians 5:3** And I testify again to every man who becomes circumcised that he is a debtor to keep the whole law.
> **James 2:10** For whoever shall keep the whole law, and yet stumble in one *point*, he is guilty of all.

Did you notice the word 'debtor'? The topic was circumcision, but the explanation is that this applies to trying to keep the Law. The Gentile Christians were being told that they were saved by Jesus, but now had to keep the Law. The concept is Jesus + law = righteousness. The early church was being infiltrated by those who were teaching that Jesus empowers us to keep the Law so we can become righteous by human efforts. This is completely false. The message of the gospel is that the Law put us in debt because every sin must pay the penalty of sin, but Jesus has made us free from the Law and its debt. We were crucified with Christ and made alive in the Spirit. He who has died has been set free from the Law.

To turn back to the Law is to willingly put ourselves back under its system of debt. Then if we offend the Law in any area, we are guilty and under its debt again. Why would the Christian want to submit back under that system?

Let's go further and look at how placing ourselves back under the Law excludes us from the promise. Look now at **Galatians 4:21-26**

> [21] Tell me, you who desire to be under the Law, do you not hear the Law?
> [22] For it is written that Abraham had two sons: the one by a bondwoman, the other by a freewoman.
> [23] But he *who was* of the bondwoman was born according to the flesh, and he of the freewoman through promise,
> [24] which things are symbolic. For these are the two covenants: the one from Mount Sinai which gives birth to bondage, which is Hagar--
> [25] for this Hagar is Mount Sinai in Arabia, and corresponds to Jerusalem which now is, and is in bondage with her children--
> [26] but the Jerusalem above is free, which is the mother of us all.

What a powerful message! The Old Testament uses real people to unveil God's purposes for us in the New Testament. When God made the covenant with Abraham, God swore that he would give Abraham the son of promise. That son would be through Sarah, even though she was barren and advanced in age.

Years passed, and Abraham and Sarah never saw the promise fulfilled, so they decided to fulfill God's promise by human effort. She took her slave, Hagar, and gave her to Abraham as a second wife. Hagar conceived and bore a son. She was still a slave, and God used this human effort as an example for us today. Ismael, Hagar and Abraham's son, was called the son of bondage, for he was born into slavery.

Several years later, God visited Abraham to fulfill the promise, and Sarah soon became pregnant with Isaac. God declared that Isaac was the son God promised under the oath God confirmed years earlier. The son born of human effort could never be part of God's promise.

Fast forward beyond the cross of Christ and God points back to this event and says the son of bondage came from Mount Sinai. Mount Sinai was where Moses came down the mountain with the stone commandments that began the era of the Law. Then the Bible makes two comparisons – Jerusalem under the Law is actually the son of bondage, but Jerusalem above is free. Jerusalem above is referring to God's people who have entered the promise of Christ. It gets better. Look now at **Galatians 4:28-31**

> [28] Now we, brethren, as Isaac *was*, are children of promise.
>
> [29] But, as he who was born according to the flesh then persecuted him *who was born* according to the Spirit, even so *it is* now.
>
> [30] Nevertheless what does the Scripture say? "Cast out the bondwoman and her son, for the son of the bondwoman shall not be heir with the son of the freewoman."
>
> [31] So then, brethren, we are not children of the bondwoman but of the free.

We'll deal with the children of the Law persecuting those of the promise in a later chapter, but I want to focus on one important truth. Those born under bondage are cast out and can never inherit the promise. Do you grasp the magnitude of that truth? Any who are under the Law cannot be an heir of God's promise. The inheritance of the Christian is ONLY by promise and can never be inherited through the Law.

Keep in mind that this explanation begins with the question, "You who desire to be under the Law, do you not hear the Law?" This was written to a group of Christians who were being told that to serve God they must keep the Law. The explanation is that those who submit back under the Law are putting themselves under the weight of debt, and cannot inherit the promise.

What did Isaac have to do to inherit the promise? He was an heir and did nothing to merit it. The son of bondage was sent away and Isaac received everything his father possessed. It's no accident that Isaac is the silent heir of the Bible. There is very little information about the life of Isaac, for his role in scripture was to be an heir of the promise.

Our inheritance is by promise through Christ. Anyone trying to advance God's will by human effort is falling into the trap of Hagar. The Law is a slave master. Any service done under the Law is required – not rewarded. A slave doesn't merit an inheritance. He or she is enslaved, and everything is of obligation and has no reward. The slave can only work to avoid the consequences of failing.

What if a Christian has submitted back to the Law? The Bible says that person is a debtor to the Law and has fallen from grace.[98] Galatians goes on to explain that when someone tries to advance grace by the efforts of the Law, "a little leaven leavens the whole lump."[99] Leaven is when yeast is added to bread dough. In this era, people would save a piece of dough from a previous lump, then add a small amount to the new lump of dough. Within a few hours, the entire lump of dough is filled with yeast and becomes leavened.

The message is that when you add works of the Law to grace, you no longer have grace, but law. The entire work of God is transformed into a human effort and Christ's completed work is pushed aside. The Bible then says, "This persuasion [to introduce human effort and the Law] does not come from Him who called you."[100] If this teaching doesn't come from God who called you, what is the only other source? It's a deception of the enemy who is persuading you to trust in something other than Christ.

---

[98] Galatians 5:3-4
[99] Galatians 5:9
[100] Galatians 5:8

This warning to the church is not a fatalistic condemnation. The church is being warned so they recognize the truth and turn their focus back to Christ. Rather than picking nuggets out of the scripture, let's let the scripture provide the solution for overcoming the flesh.

The flesh tries to both keep the Law and it tries to sin. Whether we are sinning to gratify the flesh, or attempting to keep the Law, both are focused on self and have turned away from Christ. With this in mind, let's look at the call to set our eyes on the only fulfilment of righteousness - **Galatians 5:16-25**

> [16] I say then: Walk in the Spirit, and you shall not fulfill the lust of the flesh.
> [17] For the flesh lusts against the Spirit, and the Spirit against the flesh; and these are contrary to one another, so that you do not do the things that you wish.
> [18] But if you are led by the Spirit, you are not under the Law.
> [19] Now the works of the flesh are evident, which are: adultery, fornication, uncleanness, lewdness,
> [20] idolatry, sorcery, hatred, contentions, jealousies, outbursts of wrath, selfish ambitions, dissensions, heresies,
> [21] envy, murders, drunkenness, revelries, and the like; of which I tell you beforehand, just as I also told *you* in time past, that those who practice such things will not inherit the kingdom of God.
> [22] But the fruit of the Spirit is love, joy, peace, longsuffering, kindness, goodness, faith,
> [23] gentleness, self-control. Against such there is no law.
> [24] And those *who are* Christ's have crucified the flesh with its passions and desires.
> [25] If we live in the Spirit, let us also walk in the Spirit.

Why do Christians try to keep the Law? They are trying to overcome the flesh by human effort. They are trying to please God by human effort. Yet both are fulfilled in this – walk in the Spirit and you will not fulfill the lusts of the flesh. It's a guarantee.

One of the main points of the rebuttal I read was this, "It's necessary to keep the Law so we don't sin and violate God's commandments." But what does the scripture say? If you are in the Spirit, you don't even need to concern yourselves with the lust of the flesh – it is displaced because it cannot enter into our life in the Spirit or go where we are walking. The biggest affront of sin in the Christian's life is the call to cease from trusting in Christ and look to either ourselves, or back to the Law God redeemed us out of.

Let me reiterate it this way, to cease from trusting in Christ's work is the only sin we should be concerned with. If we keep the whole law by our efforts, we are still in sin, for we have declared Jesus' work as insufficient and ourselves as the creator of righteousness.

In Galatians above, a comparison is made between the flesh and the Spirit. "The works of the flesh are these..." then every sin we need to avoid is listed. But where do these emerge? Sin emerges when we allow the flesh to do its work. Then we are told that the Law applies to those who are in the flesh. This must be so, for in the Spirit, the Law is already fulfilled. Only the flesh can be under the Law. Working in the Law is working in the flesh. Rather than producing righteousness, we are enabling the flesh to become our trust. The end result is the flesh produces its sinful works, for the flesh cannot produce God's works.

Notice the Bible doesn't call us to the 'works' of the Spirit. It is the fruit of the Spirit. All the things we desire are not earned, worked for, or accomplished. They are fruit that naturally emerges from the life of the one who walks in the Spirit. Or as Jesus said, "If you abide in Me and I in you, you will bear much fruit, for without Me you can do nothing." Fruit is a guarantee to the person walking in the Spirit, for it is God who works in you to accomplish His will and good pleasure.[101]

You can't work for fruit, you can only abide in Christ so His life flows through you to produce the fruit of the Spirit. Do you want goodness? Self-control? Peace? Joy? A deeper faith? Stop working and start trusting and abiding.

And this is what it means to walk in the Spirit. To walk in the Spirit is to look to Christ, trust fully in His completed work, and receive His life as a free gift of grace. In 1 Corinthians 15:10, the Apostle Paul makes an interesting statement, "I labored more

---

[101] Philippians 2:13

abundantly than them all, yet it wasn't I, but the grace of God was working through me."

If you are already in the Spirit – which you are if you are in Christ – then the Bible commands that you walk in the Spirit. If you walk in the Spirit, you have already fulfilled the Law. You are in Christ, and He has fulfilled all things. As you walk in the Spirit, the fruit of the Spirit does in you what the Law could never do. The good works of God are naturally part of the life walking in the Spirit, and His grace, working in you, causes you to labor more abundantly than them all. The labors of the Law cannot measure up to the grace of God working through you.

What's more is you will rest from your labors, and good works will be refreshing instead of a burden. A friend recently said, "I'm doing less work for God, but I am more satisfied and fulfilled." I would add that he also has more fruit. It's less work because all the meaningless labors have been taken out of the way, and now he is free to walk in the works God has prepared for him. There is no burn out when we are walking in God's works.

Keeping the Law is not only unnecessary, it is a denial of Christ. Any who mix law with grace have leavened the whole lump. They are no longer holding to faith and grace, but law. The answer is to turn from the Law and trust fully in His grace. Works + Law = Law. Faith + Human Effort = Human Effort. Rest your hope fully upon God's revelation of grace and He will fulfill in you what works and religion cannot accomplish.[102]

I'll repeat this a few times in this book because it is important. Grace is the unmerited favor of God. To receive grace, we not only believe in the completed work of Christ, but we put our trust in that completed work. When you need righteousness, trust in the gift of righteousness given through Christ. When you sin, trust in His forgiveness given through the cross. When you need strength, trust in the power of His might given to you through Christ. When you feel the call of serving God, trust in the completed work of Christ and allow His grace to work through you to fulfill your calling into ministry.

---

[102] 1 Peter 1:13

Name any spiritual attribute or endeavor. It has all been given to us through Christ. We now must look expectantly to God and receive all things that pertain to life and godliness through Him. Anything from any other source is disbelief in His completed work. Grace plus law equals law. Grace plus works equals law.

Grace received by faith fulfills the Law, overcomes the flesh, and fulfills our calling. The fruit of the Spirit is God's work in you, not your spirituality accomplished for Him. In the same way, good works are not what you do for God, but the natural result of walking in the Spirit and yielding so the Lord can accomplish His work through you.

Discussion Questions:

Review Romans 10:4 and 2 Corinthians 3:5-13. For whom does the Law pass away, and why is it passing?

Review Romans 8:3-4. How is the Law fulfilled?

Do the areas in which we keep the Law merit enough righteousness to justify the areas where we disobey the Law?

Does the Law reward obedience? Why or why not?

Review Romans 3:19-20. What is the main purpose of the Law?

What is the weakness of the Law?

Read Galatians 5:16-25.
What must we do to obtain the fruit of the Spirit?

How do we bear fruit?

Does the fruit of the Spirit overcome the works of the flesh?

If the fruit of the Spirit is maturing in our lives, what happens to sin in our lives?

Is self-righteous efforts a denial of Christ? Explain.

Persecution of Grace

The Law always views grace as a threat. This is clearly seen in the Bible, in history, and also in our modern era. There are several reasons for this, most notably is this explanation from **Galatians 5:17**

> For the flesh sets its desire against the Spirit, and the Spirit against the flesh; for these are in opposition to one another, so that you may not do the things that you please. (NASB)

The flesh is opposed to the Spirit. The flesh and the Spirit can never agree because they each desire what is diametrically opposed to the other. The flesh desires control, the Spirit gives freedom. The flesh seeks to trust in itself, the Spirit puts all trust in the Lord. In the flesh is bondage, in the Spirit is liberty. The flesh masquerades itself as religion, the Spirit denies all human effort, religious or otherwise.

Remember when we looked at Peter's warning about those who promise liberty, but are slaves of corruption? In no area is this more true than in religion. All religion promises liberty, but religion itself is a form of bondage. It seeks to control the masses through both promises and fear tactics. Whereas the Spirit reveals the glory of faith so we are drawn to submit and receive from God through a joyful and willing heart. We don't submit because we are placed under the bondage of fear. We submit because we see the value of life in the Spirit. When we see the excellence of knowing Christ, everything else is revealed to be worthless by comparison.

Fear is the greatest tool of religion. People are taught to be afraid of offending God and are compelled to give more, do more, use specific styles of music, use a specific translation, and abide by many other laws out of fear of the hammer of God's wrath.

Let me give an example. Have you heard this taught? "God's going to get His money one way or another. If you don't tithe, you'll have unforeseen expenses. Your car will break down. You'll get sick and have medical bills. You may lose your job. If you don't tithe, you are robbing God and God will take from you."

If you read through the New Testament, you will not find anything that supports this belief. There is a single verse in the Bible by which this doctrine is built upon, but we are going to look at the context and not just this one verse. **Malachi 3:8-10**

> [8] "Will a man rob God? Yet you have robbed Me! But you say,'In what way have we robbed You?' In tithes and offerings.
> [9] You are cursed with a curse, For you have robbed Me, *Even* this whole nation.
> [10] Bring all the tithes into the storehouse, That there may be food in My house, And try Me now in this," Says the LORD of hosts, "If I will not open for you the windows of heaven And pour out for you *such* blessing That *there will* not *be room* enough *to receive it*.

From the context, this clearly belongs to the Old Covenant. It refers to the nation of Israel failing to abide by the Law, and it primarily focuses on food. The bulk of the tithe was from the produce of their farming. That's why it is referring to the storehouse. It was the whole nation that was condemned because the Old Covenant was to the descendants of Abraham and did not apply to any Gentile or non-Jewish nation. In fact, the only way anyone outside of Israel could get under the Old Covenant was to be circumcised and become a proselyte. A proselyte is a Gentile in the process of converting to Judaism. So even if you want to keep this commandment, you cannot do so without abandoning the covenant of grace, converting to Judaism, and placing yourself back under the Law of condemnation.

Clearly this passage cannot be kept by the Christian, for we will never be under the Law and it is a rejection of Christ's work to place ourselves under the Old Covenant. If we are going to zero in on this command, why aren't we focusing on the Old Covenant commands the condemned the Jews for buying and selling on the Sabbath? Or the commands that say those who aren't circumcised are cut off from God's covenant (Old Covenant)? If we are going to put ourselves under the Law, according to the Bible, we are debtors to keep the whole law – not just the one commandment we are focused on.

In the New Testament, giving is very much a part of the Christian life, but it is out of a joyful heart and not out of fear or obligation. In fact, the Bible condemns giving out of obligation. Here is the New Testament teaching on giving - **2 Corinthians 9:6-7**

> [6] But this *I say*: He who sows sparingly will also reap sparingly, and he who sows bountifully will also reap bountifully.
> [7] *So let* each one *give* as he purposes in his heart, not grudgingly or of necessity; for God loves a cheerful giver.

Notice one thing that is strangely absent. Where is the curse? It's not here. The truth is, if you give out of obligation, you are not giving anything God will ever honor. A grudging heart that gives is giving out of the flesh and not by faith. Anything that is not of faith is sin. The one who gives because they believe it is necessary to give is not under the blessing, but under the Law. That person should not expect to be rewarded, for deeds done under the Law are acts of the flesh outside of Christ.

There is no warning that God will get His money. There is no condemnation or judgment for those who 'violate the covenant'. The message is that we are blessed when we give out of joy, but not cursed when we don't give. The Christian cannot be cursed, for in Christ the curse of the Law has been removed. The only warning is that the one who gives little will reap little – and our reaping is not limited to only money, nor is it limited to this passing life.

We give because we are overflowing with joy for what God is doing and out of our confidence of what He is able to do. We don't give because we fear God will take it from us. We give because we trust God and believe He has called us to meet a need or support the work of someone or a ministry God is using. We give out of the joyful heart that trusts in the Lord.

Do you see the difference between the Law and the Spirit? The Law produces fear, but the Spirit produces a joyful, giving heart. One gives out of fear and obligation; the other gives out of God's bounty. The one under the Law is trying to avoid a curse. The one under grace is sharing the faith they have received from God.

There is much more we could say on giving, but the point of this chapter is to show that grace by faith is the antithesis of works by the Law. Those under the Law are offended by grace because the Law does not approve of someone's freedom to give or not to give. The Law forces behavior, but grace draws from the fulfillment of the Law through Christ. The Law says, "Give or you will be cursed." Grace says, "Only give as God has led your heart while trusting that He desires to bless all the more."

If this is true (and it is), why do people teach law? People turn to the Law when they don't trust the Spirit. Churches don't believe God will raise up people with the purpose in their hearts to give. They don't truly believe God will supply their need, so they fall back on their own works in an attempt to accomplish God's work. If someone isn't confident God is behind their work, they have to look elsewhere. If this is the case, they should consider this question, "Are they building God's Kingdom, or their own?"

Those who trust in the Law believe that giving people the option to not give is a threat. A people under grace cannot be manipulated into funding the Law; therefore, grace becomes a threat.

Those trusting in the Law believe that teaching people that all their sins are permanently taken away is a threat because people might choose to sin. True, some may indeed commit sins they would not have done, but to trust in the Law over Christ is the greater sin.

The Law says, "If you sin you will be cursed." Grace says, "The curse has been removed under Christ for all who believe. Walk in righteousness so you don't come short of any of God's promises."[103] Certainly Christians can forfeit their inheritance for the things of this life, but there is a big difference between saying that sin curses the Christian and saying that sin takes us out of God's plan of blessing. Equally problematic is when someone claims the Law gives God's blessings instead of holding to the New

---

[103] 1 Corinthians 1:7, Hebrews 4:1, Hebrews 12:15

Testament teaching that obedience leads us into God's blessings. One is an act of faith, the other is the Old Covenant threat of fear.

The Old Covenant warned of the curse, but in Christ, the curse has already been removed through the penalty of the cross. By faith, we have been crucified with Christ; therefore, in Him we died to both the Law and the curse of the Law. In Christ there can be no curse of the Law.

Faith believes in God's promises so we value what lies ahead more than the world we are leaving behind. Law and legalism tries to protect us from sin by rules and regulations. Grace invites us into a better way. One warns us of a curse; the other says the curse has been done away with, now look how much greater things await to those who trust God. One uses fear to manipulate conformity, the other reveals the promise through the invitation of walking in the Spirit.

There will always be those who attempt to turn the grace of God into a selfish gospel. The apostles even addressed this.[104] The Bible says that the way of truth will be maligned because of those who use only the scriptures that can be twisted into self-justification for a sinful lifestyle.[105] We see this today. People who oppose the grace of God point to those who do not understand grace as the reason for their opposition to God's way of truth. The way of truth may indeed be blasphemed as the Bible foretold, but that doesn't make the way of truth wrong.

Both those who use grace as justification for sin, and those who use sin as justification for returning to the Law are equally wrong. Don't allow yourself to be drawn away from truth because someone lives contrary to it.

Those who trust the Law are also trusting in what Christ has taken out of the way, and this compels them to oppose those who trust fully in Christ. This is so because those who trust in God's grace are no longer honoring the object of the legalist's faith. This goes back to the first murder.

---

[104] Jude 1:4
[105] 2 Peter 2:2

Remember Cain and Able? Why did Cain hate Able? Cain worked his heart out producing the best fruits of his labors. He brought all his hard work to God and God rejected it. Cain represents legalism. He did everything that looks right according to the highest religious standard, but his righteousness could never measure up to God's standard.

The man of grace was Able. Able trusted in God's works. God provided Able with an acceptable sacrifice, and Able took God's provision for sin and offered it back to God. It was a foreshadow of the future blood covenant of Christ. He was trusting in God's provision for sin instead of his own merits. God accepted Able. Cain resented it. He worked circles around Able, so why should his brother be accepted and not himself?

Why did God accept Able's offering without work, but not accept Cain's offering that was born out of much hard work? It's because works have never merited God's favor.

In the Christian life, we see the same scenario played out among the brethren in Christ. There are many sincere Christians who are working their hearts out by personal striving and hard efforts. Yet they look to their brethren who say, "God has provided all things that pertain to life and godliness. I will offer back to God what He has given me. He has given me a purified heart, and I will offer back the sacrifice of praise. The only thing I can offer is gratitude for what He has done." Or as **Hebrews 13:15** says:

> Therefore by Him let us continually offer the sacrifice of praise to God, that is, the fruit of *our* lips, giving thanks to His name.

What can I offer God that He does not already possess? What works can I do that He has not already done? All I can do is walk in His works, praise what God has accomplished, and give thanksgiving for what He has given.

Yet those who cannot let go of the Law – even if that law is a revised Christian law – will be offended by the true faith of trusting in Christ's completed work. Religion stands with Cain and says, "What have you done that makes you acceptable?" Those of faith will look to Christ and say, "He has done the work. It is Christ who makes me acceptable. The only thing I can sacrifice is my praise for His work." And this attitude of true faith will always offend religion. This is especially true of the Christian religion.

Look at church history and you will find all the evidence you need. Many martyrs have come by the hand of those who claim to be followers of the Bible. Many will point to the inquisition period and look down at the Catholic religious system, but what happened during the early reformed movement? Once protestants gained power, they began persecuting both Catholics, and protestants that didn't hold to their system of religion.

Most people know the Catholic church had a system of labeling as heretics those who didn't trust in the church, and then putting them to death. What people often don't realize is that the reformers quickly adopted that same attitude. John Calvin is on record multiple times calling for the execution of any deemed as a heretic by the Protestant movement. When criticized, he said, "Whoever shall now contend that it is unjust to put heretics and blasphemers to death will knowingly and willingly incur their very guilt."[106]

Yet when the disciples were met with opposition and a Samaritan city refused to let Jesus enter the city, they asked, "Should we call fire down from heaven and destroy them as Elijah did?"

Jesus rebuked them sharply and said, "You do not know what spirit you are of. I did not come to destroy men's lives, but to save them."[107] Faith invites men into grace. Legalism attempts to force conformity, and if necessary, to destroy opposition. As it was in Jesus' day, so it is today. God rebukes those who are not of the Spirit of grace, and in order to walk with Christ, we must abandon that attitude and learn to trust in His Spirit to call any

---

[106] Letter to Farel, **20 August 1553**; in Henry Beveridge and Jules Bonnet, editors, David Constable, translator, *Selected Works of John Calvin: Tracts and Letters*: Volume 5: *Letters, Part 2: 1545-1553*; originally published in Philadelphia by Presbyterian Board of Publication, 1858; reprinted by Baker Book House, Grand Rapids, MI, 1983, p. 417
[107] Luke 9:52-56

who will come. The fact is, any who look to religion will be drawn into legalism. Any who look to Christ will be called into grace.

Works views grace as a threat. Cain focused on works, but Able rested in God's provision. When Cain's sacrifice was rejected, he looked at Able and seethed with anger. He then went after Able and killed his brother. Nothing has changed. Look again at **Galatians 4:29-31**

> [29] But, as he who was born according to the flesh then persecuted him *who was born* according to the Spirit, even so *it is* now.
> [30] Nevertheless what does the Scripture say? "Cast out the bondwoman and her son, for the son of the bondwoman shall not be heir with the son of the freewoman."
> [31] So then, brethren, we are not children of the bondwoman but of the free.

The Apostle Paul is teaching the Galatian church how to trust in the promise and not works. He asks this question, "Are you so foolish, having begun by faith, do you now believe you can be made perfect by the flesh?"[108] In other words, we received life by trusting in Christ without human effort. Do we now think the rest of the Christian life is lived by human effort? No, we live our lives the same way we entered this life – by faith in Christ.

Notice I said faith in Christ. Many walk by faith in Christian ordinances, but these are not walking in the Spirit. As it was with Cain, so it was in the early church, and so it is in our modern church culture. Those who live by works reject those who live by the promise of Christ.

Only God has the right to cast out those bound by law. Our role is not to judge who is worthy of faith, nor is it to judge those caught in legalism. Our role is to point to the finished work of Christ so people can be drawn out of the human way of religious thinking.

Those who are trying to live according to the flesh will always view those who live by the promise as a threat. Just as the Jews were very sincere, but wrong, many churches are very sincere but wrong. They persecute those who put their trust in

---

[108] Galatians 3:3

the promise, "Christ has given us all things that pertain to life and godliness." Grace is viewed as a threat, and those who walk by faith in Christ are attacked as if they were enemies of God.

It is not possible to walk in grace and be one who attacks the brethren. This is the fruit of legalism. Grace leads us to the fruit of the Spirit. Once we see the desire to judge someone as worthy or unworthy, it's a sign that we are falling back into a legalistic standard. Yes, if we make grace into a system of rules, it too becomes legalism.

At the heart of most fleshly mindedness is this – control. Leaders want to control the people. Organizations want to control churches. People want to control other people. Freedom is always a threat to control, yet the person who is walking in the Spirit cannot go far off course. Because the Spirit is leading, they will discern when they are pulling against the Spirit. This must be our trust. It's the Spirit's role to lead the heart. We can't replace the Spirit's leading with a legalistic fence of protection. The fence of rules that prevents the wandering soul is also the barrier that prevents people from following the Spirit of God.

Some will use grace as an excuse to go their own way and cast off all restraint. The Bible addresses sin in the Christian life. For some, it says, "Examine yourselves to see if you are really in the faith."[109] If someone can live counter to Christ and not feel the call to righteousness, do they truly have a new life in the Spirit? If someone does not have the life of the Spirit, forcing them into conformity with rules won't change their spiritual condition. The answer is not to create rules, but to present the truth of life.

To those in Christ, the Bible constantly reminds us of what we have, what we will inherit, and the hope we are given. Then the call is, "Don't become like Esau, who forfeited his blessings to gratify the flesh."

Absent is the call to return to the Law. Absent is a revamping of a new legal system under a Christian umbrella.

True discipleship is not making someone conform through fear and manipulation. True discipleship is teaching people who

---

[109] 2 Corinthians 13:5

they are in Christ, the fellowship we have been given, and how to walk by faith in the completed work of Christ. Once someone grasps this as a reality, they are drawn into a godly lifestyle. Once someone learns how to enjoy fellowship with God, the temptations of the world lose their appeal. Take to heart the words of **Philippians 3:8-10**

> [8] Yet indeed I also count all things loss for the excellence of the knowledge of Christ Jesus my Lord, for whom I have suffered the loss of all things, and count them as rubbish, that I may gain Christ
> [9] and be found in Him, not having my own righteousness, which *is* from the Law, but that which *is* through faith in Christ, the righteousness which is from God by faith;
> [10] that I may know Him and the power of His resurrection, and the fellowship of His sufferings, being conformed to His death,

This was written by the Apostle Paul. He abandoned his religious profession. He left his successful religious career behind, all its worldly benefits, and he abandoned his reputation. He was under the most respected teachers of the day. He persecuted the church because he believed in the Law. Yet Christ changed everything. The more he gained knowledge of what he had in Christ, the more he counted everything as trash by comparison. He abandoned his own righteousness, religion, profession, and everything his life had to offer.

It wasn't fear that compelled the Apostle Paul. It was the hope before Him and the excellence of what He had discovered in Christ. No one can have this joy by anything other than trusting fully in the invitation of grace. The more he discovered about what was already His in Christ, the more passionately he pursued the life of faith and obedience.

He didn't obey because of the fear of consequences, but out of the joy of the promises of God.

Religion locks people into a sectarian mindset. If you are not familiar with that term, it means to be divided into sects. A sect is a group of people who divide from others to form their own circle. This is true for both cults, and the Christianized religious world. Sectarianism causes people to refuse to consider any scriptural truth that does not fall within the box they have established. People fear truth. Though the sectarianist doesn't believe they are rejecting the scriptures, the truth is that once they recognize they are being drawn outside of the box, they shut down and resist considering anything that does not affirm their sect or denomination. Anything that doesn't fall within the framework of their traditionally held beliefs – even if it is true – is viewed as a threat. This causes people to become rigid, legalistic, and divisive. I know this is true because I have been there.

Religion blinds the eyes of the follower. Even if someone claims to respect the Bible, it's hard to get someone to honestly look at scriptures that question their held beliefs or present truths that they have been conditioned to fear. Though a doctrine may be indefensible by scripture, because it has always been believed, that belief is held in higher regard than the word of God. That's when people become angry, confrontational, and withdraw from looking at the scriptures.

To keep people inside the box of sectarianism, fear is often employed. Every minor disagreement is exploited as if it were heresy, and once you label someone as an enemy of a Christian sect, they are then identified as an enemy of God. Then it's okay to attack them. Yet the Bible says we are to bless our enemies and never curse.[110]

> Here is a good litmus test for religion. Look at **1 John 4:16-19**
> [16] And we have known and believed the love that God has for us. God is love, and he who abides in love abides in God, and God in him.
> [17] Love has been perfected among us in this: that we may have boldness in the day of judgment; because as He is, so are we in this world.
> [18] There is no fear in love; but perfect love casts out fear, because fear involves torment. But he who fears has not been made perfect in love.
> [19] We love Him because He first loved us.

Do your beliefs teach this, "We have known and believe the love that God has for us?" Or does it focus on fearing that God is condemning any who don't adhere to religious conditions? Our faith is in His love. Otherwise, we are trusting in rules and conditional acceptance.

---

[110] Matthew 5:44, Romans 12:14

What's more is that perfect love casts out all fear. If you are truly walking by faith, you have the promise, "Love (agape) has been perfected among us." Us is the church. If you are in the promise that love has been perfected among us, then you have also the promise that this perfect love casts out all fear.

The one who fears has not been perfected in love. This person is not believing in the love God has revealed, but is stuck in the legalistic mindset of conditional love – which is not love at all. If you are afraid God has rejected you, or may reject you, you have not yet trusted in the perfecting love of God. When you have faith and trust in God's love given to you, all fear is cast out and you are as He is in this world.[111] You will share that same love with others and will never again fear failure or the loss of God's approval.

And what is everything based upon? He first loved you. God is not saying, "Love me and I will accept you." God is not responding to our love. We are responding to His love. He first loved us, poured His love into our hearts by the Holy Spirit,[112] and we trust in that love and are established with confidence in what He has given us. We are then able to love God with the perfect love His Spirit places within us. It can't work the other way around. No one loves God by human effort, for human love is never perfect.

Whatever is not of love persecutes that which is born out of God's love. Yet we are called to return a blessing for the curse. We are commanded to not be distracted by the warnings of fear, for we are perfected by God in His love. Trust in God's love; not in the fear of religion. Then don't be surprised if religion views your trust in Christ's completed work as a threat. However, in the end, love will stand with confidence in judgment. Religion and fear will not.

---

[111] 1 John 4:17
[112] Romans 5:5

Discussion Questions

Read Galatians 3:10-14. Under Christ, can we be cursed? Why or why not?

According to this passage, who is under the curse?

Why does common Christianity focus on fear and consequences?

If someone is walking by faith, do they need fear as a motivator?

Can fear create true obedience?

Does fear support or undermine faith?

Is it the church's job to make sure people don't sin?

Read Titus 2:11-12. What teaches people to deny ungodliness and walk in righteousness?

Why does legalism persecute faith?

How do we love God?

What draws people out of sin?

Why do people lose their love for the world?

Can grace be abused?

Do we need to protect grace?

Grace – The Reception of Perfection

God has designed us to not be content with the temporal – for we are created with eternity in our hearts. Take **Ecclesiastes 3:11** to heart:
> He has made everything beautiful in its time. Also He has put eternity in their hearts, except that no one can find out the work that God does from beginning to end.

Life is much more than existing or pursuing the things that have no lasting value. People are discontent because everything they value is passing away. How can we have significance in life by loving and pursuing things that have no eternal significance? Deep in the heart of every man or woman, God has placed a longing for the eternal. Since we have been designed for eternity, nothing in life can fill the void God has placed within us – except Him.

You were created for fellowship with God, and everything in life is designed to bring that purpose into the reality of your life. Everything is beautiful in its time; therefore, the only reason something becomes harmful is when it is taken outside of God's eternal design and made into a pursuit to only gratify temporal flesh. Only when eternity is pushed aside does God's design become corrupted and sinful.

This should also give you great comfort, for if God's purpose is to bring you into the knowledge of His fellowship, He works to remove anything that prevents you from enjoying that fellowship. We have liberty with anything that God does not expressly state as something which prevents us from enjoying fellowship with Him. Nothing is sinful until it becomes the object of our affection instead of God. When our focus is stuck on temporal things of this life, God works to remove these harmful barriers. This includes your focus on sin. Your failures are not barriers to God's purpose of fellowship. Every failure, regardless of how regretful it may be on your part, is resolved by His work on your behalf. God asks for one thing from you. Let's look at Jesus' own words in **John 6:28-29**

²⁸ Then they said to Him, "What shall we do, that we may work the works of God?"
²⁹ Jesus answered and said to them, "This is the work of God, that you believe in Him whom He sent."

The people of Jesus' day were looking at human effort. They wanted to know what they must do to please God. The answer to their question is the answer to all the Christian's struggles. It's not your work, it's God's work. You are only asked to believe on Christ, who accomplished the works of God.

One of the apostles of Jesus always referred to himself as 'the disciple Jesus loved'. This was John. You find John close to Jesus, and four times he refers to himself as the one Jesus loved. Is it any wonder he felt close to the Lord? What prevented others from drawing near? Jesus didn't love John more, John simply believe Christ loved Him and therefore experienced the depth of that love.

Everything in scripture pours out the evidence that God loves you with incomprehensible love. Every barrier has been removed between us and God, and nothing is based on what we accomplished for Him. God has given us the evidence of love through Christ, through His promises, through the constant affirmation of the Spirit within us, and through His continuous guiding hand. The only barrier is your misconceptions of His intentions. If you don't trust His love, you naturally resist His fellowship.

The church is stuck in the mindset of trying to measure up to a false expectation of God. Yet God knows we are limited and He knows that the weakness of the Law is us – those born in the flesh. And He is not concerned with our inabilities. He created us with limitations so we would not lose sight of our Creator. Your limitations and weaknesses serve no other purpose than to reveal God's perfect love.

Stop for a moment and meditate on this truth. Consider the weaknesses of your life. Think about the things you are ashamed of. Think about the sins that habitually defeat you. Think about the things that make you feel like God is angry or disappointed in you. These weaknesses and failures cannot destroy you. They cannot overthrow the love of God or the work of Christ. These limitations are the evidences of God's love. It's God's way of proving to you that you don't have to prove yourself to Him. These human limitations are necessary, for it shows us that God's love is unconditional.

He knew you before you were born, yet still loved you and used your failures as opportunities to reveal His strength and love. As you are established in His love, God then overcomes your weaknesses with His holiness. Sin is not defeated before you come to Him. God accepts you and I as we are, and then He becomes the one who overcomes our weaknesses, removes our sin, and He becomes our perfection.

If you could be perfect, then it might be valid to believe God's love was a conditional response to your achievement. But when you can't do anything for God, it is then that you fully recognize that God's love is not performance based, but is the perfect expression of God's nature. The Bible says that God is love. Because He is love, love must express itself as an act of grace. Look at **1 John 4:16**

> And we have known and believed the love that God has for us. God is love, and he who abides in love abides in God, and God in him.

Stop and meditate on the power of this passage. Do you believe God is love? At the center of a guilty conscience is a heart that does not believe this. Shame becomes the evidence that we don't know and believe in the love of God. Legalism is the active expression of disbelief in the truth that God is love.

How do we have fellowship with God – perfect fellowship? Why was John able to always be right beside Christ? It was because he truly believed in the love of God. He knew he was loved, and it drew him close.

You abide in God by abiding in His love. You abide in His love by knowing and believing in the love He has for you. It is you, the individual, God loves. You are the disciple God loves. Until you believe this, you will always stand aloof and miss the reality of perfect fellowship.

He who fears has not been perfected in love.[113] Very few Christians truly believe in the love of God. They trust in their performance, and when their efforts fall short or they stumble out of the standard of perfection, they feel God's love withdraw from them. But it isn't God's love withdrawing; it is their disbelief persuading them to withdraw from God.

Your efforts cannot overcome anything. It can only distract you from the true power of the Christian life – faith – trusting fully in the love of God and all He has done for us. Take to heart **1 John 5:4-5**

> [4] For whatever is born of God overcomes the world. And this is the victory that has overcome the world-- our faith.
> [5] Who is he who overcomes the world, but he who believes that Jesus is the Son of God?

What overcomes the world? Our obedience? Our works? Our own righteousness? There is only one victory – our faith. Your faith. And what is faith? It is believing that Jesus is the Son of God who has accomplished all things for us. He overcame and has given us His work. Look at **John 16:33**

> "These things I have spoken to you, that in Me you may have peace. In the world you will have tribulation; but be of good cheer, I have overcome the world."

This was spoken just before Jesus was arrested and crucified. Many years later, John looked back at this and fully understood that because Jesus overcame, we have overcome when we trust in Him.

And this is the message of grace. Grace is the completed work of Christ, which fulfilled the Law, accomplished righteousness, took away sin, revealed the love of God, and gave us all things that pertain to life and godliness. We now trust in His grace and receive all of these gifts of love. They were given to us with the gift of God's perfect love. By faith, you trust in God's love and receive these gifts of favor into your life.

---

[113] 1 John 4:18

Everything eternal has already been given to you and me. As we grow in faith, we are learning to receive from God's hand as we trust in His works, and let go of our own. Once you believe in His completed work, you will walk in the victory that overcomes the world.

God is not asking anything of you except to trust in Him. God is asking you to turn from your own ways and efforts, and to receive His love into your life. Faith understands that receiving God's work is what transforms us from failure to victory, from death to life, from guilt to peace, and from regret to joy. Once you understand that Christ's victory is your victory, all your failures will become irrelevant. Once you understand that the completed work of Christ is God's gift of righteousness to you, all your works will also become irrelevant.

Grace is not merely believing that God is good and favors us. It's to have faith in His good work. Faith is when we see the works of God, believe in it, put our trust in what He has done, and receive it into our lives.

Experiencing grace is an act of faith. It is to look expectantly to God and receive Christ as our life. We must not have a passive observation of grace, but the active receiving of grace. Faith without works is dead, being alone. To say, "I believe," means nothing. Living faith sees the work of God and draws us to actively walk in God's grace – which is His completed work, given to us as a gift of His love. That's what it means to abide in the love of God.

Let's take a moment to revisit **Hebrews 11:6**

But without faith *it is* impossible to please *Him*, for he who comes to God must believe that He is, and *that* He is a rewarder of those who diligently seek Him.

Are you rewarded for what you have done? For being sinless? For being in the right denomination? Your only call is to believe. The person who believes God is drawn to diligently seek Him. We seek because we know the treasure is before us. The reward is not only heaven – it is our daily life of joy in the love of God.

If someone hid a bar of gold in your yard and said, "It's yours if you take it," how long would you seek it? You would seek until you found it. If you didn't find what you were looking for right away, you wouldn't give up. Once you are certain it is there, you will seek until you find it. The more you have to seek, the greater the joy you'll feel when you find it.

We have the promise of all things that pertain to life and godliness. All things that apply to this life and the eternal life to come are already ours. Yet why don't people find this victory? Why are people struggling to figure out this Christian life? Why do people get frustrated and give up? It's because they don't truly believe God has given them all things. They seek without expectation, then quickly give up and turn to their own resources. The old life that couldn't give them salvation becomes the broken tool people trust in to find righteousness and spiritual significance.

This is the victory that overcomes the world, our faith. Not our works. Faith in Christ. The problem is that people trust more in themselves and their efforts than in Christ. If your efforts couldn't perfect you before you came to Christ, why would you trust in the flesh and human effort to accomplish the works of God? And these are the same works that God has already accomplished. Take to heart the words of Jesus in **Matthew 7:7-11**

> [7] "Ask, and it will be given to you; seek, and you will find; knock, and it will be opened to you.
> [8] "For everyone who asks receives, and he who seeks finds, and to him who knocks it will be opened.
> [9] "Or what man is there among you who, if his son asks for bread, will give him a stone?
> [10] "Or if he asks for a fish, will he give him a serpent?
> [11] "If you then, being evil, know how to give good gifts to your children, how much more will your Father who is in heaven give good things to those who ask Him!

Each of these, seek, knock, and ask are in the present active tense in the original Greek. It isn't just to seek, but to seek and keep seeking. It's to ask and keep asking. Knock and keep knocking. Each of these are acts of expectation. It is to seek, ask, and knock with the full expectation of receiving the full grace of God promised to you.

Don't allow your focus to be limited to gratifying the flesh. Satisfaction is not found by asking for the world and temporary pleasures. The above promise draws us to be seeking, asking, and knocking with the eternal perspective. James 4 says the reason we don't receive is because we are seeking to fulfill the flesh. A fleshly minded Christian is missing the whole message of life. God will indeed cover our lives with good things that are for this life only, but our focus is never for this life only. The river of God's pleasures is for those who trust under the shadow of His wings.[114]

The message is that we seek God's kingdom and His righteousness, and trust that God will add the things of this life to us.[115] Seek God, not the flesh. Diligently seeking God is the meaning of life. Seeking this life only creates emptiness, but seeking God satisfies the soul, sets our heart on the treasures of the next life, *and* satisfies this life also. Seeking the world creates emptiness, but seeking the Lord blesses us on both sides. Even a poor man is abundantly satisfied when he learns to abide in the love of God.

Whether our life is filled with temporary possessions or not, this world is irrelevant and we know God will only provide what is good. Our economic status is not the measure of God's favor.

If there is one thing I hope you take from this book is this: trust fully in Christ's completed work, and receive all things by faith. When you fail, receive His victory. When you sin, receive His righteousness. When you feel the call to ministry, receive and walk in His works. Believe the promise that all things that pertain to life and godliness are gifts of God, and receiving them is to receive God's grace. Trust in Him and be a partaker of His nature. Believe God, trust in His love, and abide in it.

Walking in the Spirit is to walk by faith – trusting in God's works and receiving all things from Him –whether it be life in this

---

[114] Psalm 36:7-8
[115] Matthew 6:33, Luke 12:31

world or our desire to live in godliness. It's all about receiving and abiding in what Christ has done.

Discussion Questions

If God made all things beautiful, what makes something a sin?

Is your sin a barrier to God? Why or why not?

How does God use our failures to reveal His love?

Have you ever felt rejected by God? Does God actually reject you when you fail?

Why does the Bible tell us to know and believe in the love God has for us?

If someone doesn't believe in God's love for them, how does that affect their faith in Him?

If you firmly believe in God's love for you, how will this affect your relationship and fellowship with God?

Define grace. How do you receive grace?

Why does the seeker not always find? Why would God allow someone to seek without quickly finding?

Does seeking ever end for the Christian?

Are you the disciple God loves?

The Mind of Christ

1 Corinthians 2:15-16
> [15] But he who is spiritual judges all things, yet he himself is *rightly* judged by no one.
> [16] For "who has known the mind of the LORD that he may instruct Him?" But we have the mind of Christ.

As Christians, we have an amazing promise. You already have the mind of Christ, whether you understand this or not. Lack of understanding in this area is why most Christians miss one of the greatest benefits that accompany salvation. This also agrees with **1 John 2:27**
> But the anointing which you have received from Him abides in you, and you do not need that anyone teach you; but as the same anointing teaches you concerning all things, and is true, and is not a lie, and just as it has taught you, you will abide in Him.

It is the teaching of the Holy Spirit that guides us into an abiding relationship with Christ.

Every Christian has the anointing of Christ. This is not designated for an elite spiritual class or selected individuals. It is God who said that He is no respecter of persons, but we are all greatly beloved in His eyes. We have different gifts and callings, but one Lord and we are one body.

Though we have different gifts and callings, some gifts are common to all. There are attributes that are part of our new nature in Christ. We don't have to pray for these, seek them, work for them, or hope we are chosen by God to receive them. These gifts are already yours and waiting for you to take them up.

The anointing of the believer is one of those gifts that are a normal part of the spiritual nature given to all believers. In Romans 2, the scriptures explain to the early church (which was mostly Jewish believers) that the evidence of the Spirit can be clearly seen in those who do not have any clue about the Law – the gentiles.

Gentiles, or non-Jews, were raised without the Law. Few even knew who Moses was, much less did they have any clue about the Law, the requirements of the Law, or how to live a life of obedience. Yet the Bible points out an interesting observation. These believers, who do not have the Law, were doing by nature the things written in the Law.[116] No one was giving them a list of rules. No do's. No don'ts. No regulations. Yet they were living a lifestyle that fulfilled the Law – something even the Jews under the Law could not do.[117]

The Bible says, "They were a law unto themselves." It isn't saying that they made up their own laws, but they self-governed because something within them naturally wanted to do the things that the Old Covenant law required. Only they weren't trying to keep the Law, by nature they automatically acted in agreement with the Law.

We see the same thing with new believers today. When someone first comes to Christ, they naturally want to live according to their new nature. Sin loses its grip and they have an immediate hunger for the scriptures, and a desire to walk with God.

Unfortunately, the modern church follows the same error that plagued the early church. People are taught to begin focusing on laws – rules, regulations, do's, and don'ts. Once the focus shifts back to a standard that seeks to establish our own righteousness, we lose focus on the righteousness of Christ. We quit looking to the Spirit and start looking to people, organizations, processes, and regulations. The average Christian is taught to trust in methods and not the Spirit. People then become teacher dependent, and instead of learning how to discern the Spirit's leading, they train their minds to look to external practices and leadings.

This is why we don't understand the mind of Christ. Instead of developing a discerning mind, we develop a mind veiled to anything but church law. In fact, church law *is* the veil.

---

[116] Romans 2:14
[117] John 7:19

Go back and re-read the above passage. You are not dependent upon a person to teach you. You have the same anointing your teachers do. True discipleship based teaching should be developing believers who are Spirit led instead of people dependent. This goes against the grain of modern church thought. It also goes against the church thought that emerged in the New Testament church.

The Nicolaitan movement quickly emerged (See Revelation 2:6 and 2:15). The Nicolaitans believed that a higher class of Christian was anointed to rule over the laity and make them dependent upon leadership. That is what Nicolaitan means. It's two Greek words combined which literally means rulers over the laity. God declared that He hates this doctrine. This is also why so many books of the Bible correct this erroneous way of thinking, which distracts people from a Christ focused life of walking by faith.

In this chapter, I hope to convince you to reverse this way of thinking so you can begin developing a mind that receives from the mind of Christ and trusts in the discernment of the Holy Spirit. Keep in mind, the Spirit is always in agreement with the word of God, for God is not the author of confusion. What the Spirit reveals is always based on what the Spirit has already revealed through the prophets, those whom God used to pen the scriptures.

The church is afraid of releasing the members of the body into the trust of the Holy Spirit. However, we can't deny the Spirit the right to develop believers into maturity simply because some may wander off into the dictates of their own heart. Stunting the growth of the body in order to avoid injury is not faith. Add to this, if we are honest, everyone has flawed beliefs to varying degrees. Yet the Bible has an answer to this as well. Look at **2 Timothy 3:16-17**

> [16] All Scripture *is* given by inspiration of God, and *is* profitable for doctrine, for reproof, for correction, for instruction in righteousness,
> [17] that the man of God may be complete, thoroughly equipped for every good work.

Once again, man is used in the general sense. It is the word 'anthropos', which means human beings, both male and female. Ladies, this applies just as much to you as to the men.

As we study the scriptures, it corrects our errors, reproves our incorrect ways of thinking, instructs us into the right way, and provides good doctrine. Doctrine simply means the teaching of scripture. You study, meditate, and prayerfully seek God through the scriptures, and the Holy Spirit teaches you all things.

The Christian's doctrine should be constantly growing and improving. Our life experiences, influences, past teachings, and current teachings can influence how we interpret scripture. Yet the more we are in the word, the more truth emerges and misconceptions fall away.

God reveals truth to us, then we grow in this truth. Later, as deeper things are revealed, we may realize that our doctrine wasn't based on a full understanding. Then we add new revelation to what we already know, and sometimes that means misconceptions will be pushed aside. Sometimes those misconceptions are commonly held beliefs we have been taught. But as we grow deeper, we see where incorrect believing is a hindrance to a deeper walk of faith.

If you've read my earlier books, you will likely see a continuous transformation of my understanding. I'll give one example that clearly comes to mind. I taught (and even wrote) that God will never give you more than you can bear. It's a commonly held belief and sounds reasonable. But as I learned about how God calls us to overcome the flesh, I soon saw the Bible's teaching that the flesh is broken so we are weaned off the flesh and onto a dependence upon the Spirit. This is a natural growing process in the Christian life.

Once I received a clearer understanding, I realized that God will indeed put more on us than we can bear. He does provide a way of escape, but that escape is not through the flesh, but through allowing God to break the flesh so that our strength is in God alone. Sometimes the flesh has to be broken, and we'll keep living according to the flesh until circumstances become more than we can manage on our own. As long as I can keep winning the battle in the flesh, I will stay dependent upon the flesh. God will allow circumstances to become overwhelming in the flesh *as* He calls us to let go and trust Him. A broken life in the flesh becomes the invitation to walk by faith in the Spirit. Then true victory comes into view.

In the past I encouraged people to 'hang in there', but now I teach to let go and begin trusting. Our problems might be the call to overcome the flesh by putting our trust in the Lord and to walk by faith instead of by sight. Hopefully this example shows that a doctrine that seems reasonable may change as God reveals deeper truths that exposes human thinking and replaces it with the revelation of the deep things of God.

I'm concerned when I read authors whose doctrine never seems to grow. I begin wondering if they are actually learning, or are they resting on what they think they know. The Apostle Paul said it best, "If anyone thinks he knows anything, he knows nothing that he ought to know."[118] In other words, God's ways are unsearchable. No matter how much you now know, you haven't even scratched the surface. As long as you think you have obtained, you will not grow. And you are missing out on the depths of what God is waiting to reveal to you.

And this is what the mind of Christ is all about. The Spirit knows all things and searches the deep things of God for the purpose of revealing them to us.[119] Do you constantly experience the revelation of God to you? It should be a never ending process of growing. When we are not growing, the barrier is not on God's end.

The Communion of the Spirit

One of the wonderful truths of Christianity is that you have fellowship with God on a continual basis. Understanding the

---

[118] 1 Corinthians 8:2
[119] 1 Corinthians 2:10

spiritual reality of our faith is vital to establishing our minds in the Spirit.

There is a teaching that seems to be growing in popularity that misses the beauty of our fellowship. This teaching is that our spirit is the Holy Spirit. Not only is this false, but it misses the great work God has given to us. Our spirit is in communion with the Lord. Our spirit is a partaker of God's nature, but we are a created spiritual man and are not God Himself. Consider **2 Corinthians 5:17**
> Therefore, if anyone *is* in Christ, *he is* a new creation; old things have passed away; behold, all things have become new.

When was God created? Clearly, the Bible teaches that God is uncreated, eternally existent, and every living thing draws its life from Him. However, the spirit given to us at our new birth in Christ is newly created. The old nature was buried with Christ, and a new nature is born of God as a new creation. Our spirit is eternal from this point on, but God is eternal from both past and future. Also look at **Ephesians 4:23-24**
> [23] and be renewed in the spirit of your mind,
> [24] and that you put on the new man which was created according to God, in true righteousness and holiness.

There are many other passages that speak about our new birth, new creation, and new life. Our spirit is a partaker of God's divine nature[120] but our spirit is not divine in itself.

The confusion stems from mixing passages that are communicating two related, but separate truths. The Bible not only teaches that God places a new spirit within us, but it also teaches that God's Spirit indwells the believer. Look at these two passages:
> **Romans 8:9** But you are not in the flesh but in the Spirit, if indeed the Spirit of God dwells in you. Now if anyone does not have the Spirit of Christ, he is not His.

---

[120] 2 Peter 1:4

1 Corinthians 3:16 Do you not know that you are the temple of God and *that* the Spirit of God dwells in you?

You are the temple of God. The Spirit of God, our Creator, Redeemer, Savior, and Friend, lives inside the believer. Because we have a new spirit, born of God, and the Spirit of God Himself within us, we have fellowship with God on a continual basis. Our new spirit that God has birthed in us has fellowship with the Holy Spirit placed within us. Look at these wonderful passages:

1 Corinthians 1:9 God *is* faithful, by whom you were called into the fellowship of His Son, Jesus Christ our Lord.

1 John 1:3 that which we have seen and heard we declare to you, that you also may have fellowship with us; and truly our fellowship *is* with the Father and with His Son Jesus Christ.

In 1 John 1, we read the letter of this apostle as he invites unbelievers to trust in Christ so they can have fellowship with us, the children of God. Not only that, but he goes on to explain that the Christian also has fellowship with the Father and the Son. So we see the Bible says that we have the Holy Spirit within us, the Father within us, and the Son. All that God is now has perfect fellowship with our new man, who was created by Christ and abides in Christ.[121]

Let's dig a little deeper. The human way of thinking is that when I act contrary to God, that fellowship is broken. This is false. My mind may be in the flesh, but my spirit is always in Christ.[122] Your new nature never breaks fellowship, for that nature is in God and is incorruptible. Look at these two passages:

1 Peter 1:23 having been born again, not of corruptible seed but incorruptible, through the word of God which lives and abides forever,

1 John 3:9 Whoever has been born of God does not sin, for His seed remains in him; and he cannot sin, because he has been born of God.

---

[121] Ephesians 2:10
[122] Colossians 3:3

Did you catch the main point here? The new nature that was born of God is incorruptible. Reason should compel us to this realization, for how can anything be in God that has corruption? It cannot, for sin cannot stand in God's presence. If it could, God would have just patched up our old nature instead of burying it and giving birth to a new nature.

According to both the Apostle John and the Apostle Peter, your new nature cannot partake of corruption and therefore cannot sin. Why can't it sin? Because it is born of God. Whatever is of God is perfect and sinless. Whatever is in Christ is also perfect through Him and sinless.

We confuse the flesh with our nature, but they are separate and incompatible. The Bible says that our bodies groan while waiting for the full adoption, that time when our bodies will be transformed from corruptible to incorruptible,[123] but in this life, the flesh is still the flesh. The spirit we have from God is not of the flesh and cannot be touched by the flesh. It has perfect fellowship with God, even when our minds are stuck in the flesh.

And this brings us back to our main subject – the mind of Christ. It is necessary to understand who we are, our fellowship in the Spirit, and the division between the flesh and our spirit before we can comprehend spiritual mindedness. As long as we are looking at life through the flesh, the revelation of God will evade us and we'll miss out on the joy of our fellowship with God.

The Revelation of the Spirit

Let's begin this section by examining **Romans 8:6-10**
⁶ For to be carnally minded *is* death, but to be spiritually minded *is* life and peace.
⁷ Because the carnal mind *is* enmity against God; for it is not subject to the Law of God, nor indeed can be.
⁸ So then, those who are in the flesh cannot please God.
⁹ But you are not in the flesh but in the Spirit, if indeed the Spirit of God dwells in you. Now if anyone does not have the Spirit of Christ, he is not His.

---

[123] Romans 8:23

> [10] And if Christ *is* in you, the body *is* dead because of sin, but the Spirit *is* life because of righteousness.

The mind can be either spiritually focused, or carnal (fleshly) focused. Our minds can draw from our human will, or the revelation of God's Spirit. This is confusing to a lot of people if they don't understand that our minds can be influenced by both the flesh and our spirit. This is why the Bible says, "Trust in the Lord with all your heart and do not lean on your own understanding."[124]

Those who draw understanding from their own resources are limited to what the flesh can provide. This is why there is a way that seems right, but the end is the way of destruction.[125] Your mind is drawing its influence from either the physical world or the spiritual. And this is where the Christian separates from the rest of the world. We have the mind of Christ through the Holy Spirit within us. Our new spirit is in fellowship with the Holy Spirit, and the spiritually minded person begins to discern the mind of Christ and receive the revelation of God.

Let me qualify what is meant by spiritually minded. Many religions are spiritually minded in a worldly sense. They believe in spiritual things, but those spiritual things are based on drawing from the flesh, a leader, a spirit guide, or any number of things other than Christ. In fact, we are commanded to test the spirits to see if they are of God. We test by comparing what claims to be spiritual against the word of God. This is explained in **1 Corinthians 14:31-33**

> [31] For you can all prophesy one by one, that all may learn and all may be encouraged.
> [32] And the spirits of the prophets are subject to the prophets.
> [33] For God is not *the author* of confusion but of peace, as in all the churches of the saints.

A few nuggets of truth apply to our topic of discussion here. Notice that each person in the church can prophesy, or speak the

---

[124] Proverbs 3:5
[125] Proverbs 14:12, Proverbs 16:25

truth of God. Prophecy doesn't mean predicting the future. It means proclaiming the truth of God. The heart of prophecy is explained in Revelation 19:10, "The testimony of Jesus is the spirit of prophecy."

Every true prophecy agrees with what the prophets have already given (the spirit of the prophets) and will ultimately testify to the glory of Christ. If someone's revelation does not agree with scripture and / or does not glorify Christ, it is a false spirit. Sometimes that false spirit is simply the spirit of man speaking from his own flesh.[126]

To be spiritually minded is to be in agreement with God's word, His will, and be focused on the revelation of God's Spirit within us.

The reason we don't experience the fellowship and revelation of God is because our minds are clogged with the things of the flesh. This is the normal result of living in a world corrupted by the fall. If you walk barefooted down a dusty road, your feet will get dirty, regardless of how carefully you walk. The solution isn't to curse the dirt, but to wash it off. Mourning over the soot on our feet won't clean them up. We must take water and wash the dirt away. This is exactly how we clear our minds. Look at **Titus 3:5**

> Not by works of righteousness which we have done, but according to His mercy He saved us, through the washing of regeneration and renewing of the Holy Spirit,

Our spirit is regenerated once, but our mind is constantly regenerated by putting off the old deeds of this life and renewing our mind in the Spirit. Look at **Ephesians 4:22-24**

> [22] that you put off, concerning your former conduct, the old man which grows corrupt according to the deceitful lusts,
> [23] and be renewed in the spirit of your mind,
> [24] and that you put on the new man which was created according to God, in true righteousness and holiness.

---

[126] 1 Corinthians 2:11

Jesus gave a word-picture illustration of this when He washed the disciple's feet. Peter, being Peter, resisted because he thought the work of washing feet was too lowly for the Lord. Jesus answered by saying that Peter could not have part in Him unless he allowed Christ to do His work. Peter then went to the opposite extreme. "Don't just wash my feet. Wash my hands and head also." His attitude was, *wash all of me.*

What was Jesus' answer? You are already clean. Only your feet, that which is in contact with the world, needs to be washed. As a person, you are already clean.

We see a lot of common Christian thought in Peter's attitude. On one extreme, people don't want God to do the washing. We should be doing this. But unless we yield to God's care and work, we can't be part of what He is doing.

On the other extreme, we see people who recognize they have picked up dirt from this world, and they think they need to return to seek salvation or repentance again. But the answer of God is, "I have already made you clean. You only need to wash that which picks up the dirt of this world."

And this is what the renewing and washing of the Spirit is all about. It's to yield ourselves to God so we can have the dirt washed away and receive God's fellowship without hindrance.

If you are in Christ, you already have the mind of Christ, and according to 2 Peter 1:3, we have already been given all things through Christ. The only things preventing us from receiving God's abundance is our human limitations and a life crowded by the flesh. Spiritual growth slowly overcomes our limitations, but the flesh prevents us from receiving the things of God, which creates spiritual growth.

The answer to the renewing is to trust in God to wash us with the word, renew ourselves daily by reclining at His table, and allow God to clean that which has picked up dirt. Trust in Jesus' words, "You are clean because of the word I have spoken to you. You are all clean, only your feet needs to be washed." You have no right to call yourself unclean after God has declared you to be clean. Consistent renewal will keep our minds healthy and focused on faith.

Discussion Questions:

Who has the anointing of the Holy Spirit?

What are some things that prevent the Christian from growing into full maturity?

Should the Christian be dependent upon teachers and preachers for learning God's word?

Can a Christian who is learning on their own benefit from good teaching and preaching?

Does independent learning mean we are lone Christians without need of the body of Christ (the church)?

How do we have fellowship with God?

Can sin break fellowship with God? Why or why not?

Can sin become a barrier to us experiencing the joy of fellowship with God? Can fear and doubt also become barriers?

Read John 15:3-5, Acts 10:15 and 28, and 2 Peter 1:8-9.
What makes someone clean?

What needs to be cleaned in our daily Christian life?

According to 2 Peter 1:8-9, what causes people to cease from having a fruitful Christian life?

How does the Spirit reveal truth to the Christian?

If someone's mind is stuck on the flesh, will their minds be able to receive God's revelation?

When someone is fleshly minded, does the Spirit of God cease from revealing to that person's spirit, or could it be that they are blinded to God's revelation?

Can the fleshly mind receive of the Spirit?

Becoming Spiritually Minded

We've looked at the communion of the Spirit we have been given through Christ. Now let's look at how we discern between our flesh and the revelation of the Spirit.

Countless Christians are fleshly minded, but because the flesh can do things that have an appearance of godliness, they mistake carnality for spirituality. Then they act according to the flesh while believing they are obeying the Spirit. This is why so many people issue false prophecies, persecute their brethren, and act out in many harmful ways while believing they are doing God a service. Jesus even foretold this when He explained to His disciples that people will persecute them, exclude them from fellowship, and even kill in the name of God while thinking they are pleasing God.[127] The carnal mind often thinks they are defending the faith.

Not only will people persecute in the name of God, but many will also do good deeds in the name of God. Many will profess godliness, but will deny the true power of God.[128] If good deeds can be done in the name of God as false works, and evil deeds can be done in the name of God as false works, how do we know what the true heart of God is?

The answer is profoundly simple. It is what we have discussed throughout this book. Whatever is not of faith is sin. What is born of the Spirit is spiritual, but what is born from the flesh is flesh. These two cannot be mingled. Thankfully, we can learn to discern between our fleshly mind and the mind of the Spirit. Then we can walk according to God's revelation instead of the dictates of our heart.

Fleshly Minded

---

[127] John 16:2
[128] 2 Timothy 3:5

The average Christian slips into a flesh-based mindset, and because the church doesn't teach what it means to walk in the Spirit, they stay there. The fleshly minded person takes all their input through the flesh. They struggle with sin and shortcomings, but try to solve the problem through study, religious activities, and by trying harder.

Learning the scriptures and applying them through the flesh has little effect and no eternal value. It's as the Bible says about those who missed the promise. They received the same word as we do, but it didn't profit them, not being mixed with faith.[129] The Bible also describes this person as, "Always learning, but never able to come to the knowledge of the truth."[130] It is possible to have a lot of Bible knowledge and little or no true understanding. This works well in denominationalism, but does not profit in true spiritual growth. Let's review **Romans 8:6-10**

> [6] For to be carnally minded *is* death, but to be spiritually minded *is* life and peace.
> [7] Because the carnal mind *is* enmity against God; for it is not subject to the Law of God, nor indeed can be.
> [8] So then, those who are in the flesh cannot please God.
> [9] But you are not in the flesh but in the Spirit, if indeed the Spirit of God dwells in you. Now if anyone does not have the Spirit of Christ, he is not His.
> [10] And if Christ *is* in you, the body *is* dead because of sin, but the Spirit *is* life because of righteousness.

In this passage we see that to be carnally minded is death. The flesh is dead to God. Before coming to Christ we were dead to God. Through Christ, we died to the flesh so we could be made alive to God. Why then would we want to draw our understanding from the dead flesh? Many continue to submit their minds back into the way of death and never come to the true knowledge of the life they have been given.

The person without revelation looks to their flesh for understanding. The flesh loves to do religious things, for it masks the emptiness of life in this world through dead works. If

---

[129] Hebrews 4:2
[130] 2 Timothy 3:7

someone knows no other way, all they can do is lean on their own understanding, read the Bible with eyes of the flesh, and try to shape this world into a mock-godly standard.

Unfortunately, whatever comes through the flesh is polluted by the flesh. Jesus said, "The flesh profits nothing." Your best spiritual efforts through the flesh is worthless in the eternal life of the Spirit.

Add to this, the flesh feeds our minds with its selfishness and corrupt ways of thinking. Bitterness is masked as righteous indignation, self-glorification is masked as good works, prayer is centered upon human desires, and the list goes on and on. Yet because few Christians have any other point of reference, they continue to try to conform the flesh to an incompatible spiritual standard, and then trust the flesh to give us spiritual advice. It's no wonder Christians struggle so much to find victory in their walk of faith. It isn't based on faith. At least not faith in the right thing. We are trusting in the flesh instead of the Spirit.

Spiritually Minded

To be spiritually minded is life and peace. What a promise! This is where the rubber meets the road. The spiritually minded believer looks expectantly to the Lord for understanding, trusts the discernment of the Spirit, and learns how to receive revelation through the communion between our spirit and the Spirit of God within us.

You already have the mind of Christ. This is a fact. You already have received all things that pertain to life and godliness. This also is a fact. Consider this passage from **1 John 2:20-21**

> [20] But you have an anointing from the Holy One, and you know all things.
> [21] I have not written to you because you do not know the truth, but because you know it, and that no lie is of the truth.

How can the Bible say that we know all things? Why is the church being called to teach the truth to those who have already received it? It isn't because they don't know it, but because they DO know it. Strange? Not if you understand what is being said.

Where does that truth come from? You have the anointing of the Holy Spirit that teaches you all things. You have the mind of Christ. You have received all things by becoming a partaker of God's divine nature. Yet the Bible also states that faith comes by hearing the word of God.

The truth has to make it from our spirit to our mind. Something has to transfer the knowledge of the mind of Christ to our conscious mind. Remember the earlier passage we looked at? Where those who knew nothing about the Law, by nature, kept the things written in the Law? What revealed the Law to these people? They had the mind of Christ, knew all things, and began living by what God was revealing to them.

Unfortunately, if you fast forward a few years by reading the later letters to the churches, such as Corinthians and Galatians, a change takes place in the gentile churches. People begin walking according to the flesh and began introducing religious ordinances into their faith. The focus shifted from trusting in the Spirit of God to trusting in ordinances and the teachers who came in to teach a legalistic Christianity.

The mind looking away from Christ is in the flesh by default. The mind in the flesh cannot comprehend the truth of God. The flesh cannot fulfill the Christian walk. Nor can the flesh understand it. Look again at **Romans 8:7-9**

> [7] Because the carnal mind *is* enmity against God; for it is not subject to the Law of God, nor indeed can be.
>
> [8] So then, those who are in the flesh cannot please God.
>
> [9] But you are not in the flesh but in the Spirit, if indeed the Spirit of God dwells in you. Now if anyone does not have the Spirit of Christ, he is not His.

If you belong to Christ, your inner man is already in the Spirit. Now you must learn to walk according to the inner man and not the flesh. **Galatians 5** explains:

> [16] I say then: Walk in the Spirit, and you shall not fulfill the lust of the flesh.

...
²⁵ If we live in the Spirit, let us also walk in the Spirit.

A Christian's mind, if it is in the flesh, cannot comprehend the way of faith. If the carnal (or fleshly) mind cannot please God, what happens in the life of the Christian who is trying to live out their faith by human effort? Or what happens if we study the scriptures and draw only from human understanding? You will only have fleshly minded understanding. But as a Christian, you are not in the flesh. Stop trying to live by the flesh and look to the Spirit of God that is in everyone who belongs to Christ. Review this passage from **1 Corinthians 2:10-11**

> ¹⁰ But God has revealed *them* to us through His Spirit. For the Spirit searches all things, yes, the deep things of God.
> ¹¹ For what man knows the things of a man except the spirit of the man which is in him? Even so no one knows the things of God except the Spirit of God.

Humanity can only discern what man already knows. But those who look to the Spirit discover all that God is revealing to them. God wants you to know Him. He wants you to discover the deep things of the Spirit. He is already revealing these things to you. Or perhaps I should say, "He has already revealed them to us through His Spirit." It's a done deal. But because we have put our minds onto a fleshly way of thinking, we have limited ourselves to only knowing what man can comprehend. The fleshly minded Christian has little more understanding than those who are unbelievers. That's why so many fall back to a carnal way of living.

Most Christians stop their growth early in the faith. What was revealed at the new birth and shortly afterward is all the revelation they have received. And much of that is mixed with life experiences and poor teaching, and not fully discerned according to the life of faith.

But we have better things awaiting. Once we recognize the problem of living and thinking through the flesh, we can begin seeking God through the Spirit. As we learn to trust in God and look to receive revelation, our mind is enlightened with His truth and our understanding begins to grow.

Faith comes by hearing the word of God because when we hear the word, it begins to shift our minds to look to the Spirit, and God opens our eyes to see what He is revealing.

Here is what most people do with the word of God. They hear or read a passage and then say, "What does my Bible commentary say?" Or, "What does my preacher say?" We begin to crowd out the revelation of God and replace it with focusing on other people, other writings, or denominational boundaries. While there is nothing wrong with gleaning from good teachers who are learning from the Spirit, do not make them replacements for the Spirit's gift of understanding. God indeed reveals things to you that He will not reveal to me, and things to me that He has not revealed to you. It's called the body being edified by what every member supplies.[131]

I've seen many times where the scriptures clearly corrected misconceptions in doctrine, but people trust in the teachings of a leader or denomination and distrust the prompting of the Spirit.

By all means, we should learn from each other and discuss the scriptures as we seek a better understanding, but ultimately, we must learn to trust in the anointing we have been given. The most important thing you can do is submit to the Holy Spirit and receive revelation from God. God is always revealing the truths of His word to all believers so we can experience the transforming power of His word in our lives.

Never lose sight of this one truth – the Spirit of prophecy is the testimony of Jesus.[132] Emotions can mimic the Spirit and cloud our judgment. Everyone will see their doctrine corrected from misconceptions as they grow. However, if the scriptures are the authority to correct and teach, and Jesus is the focus, even misunderstandings are limited in their impact. As we grow in maturity, we will also learn to discern between our emotions and the Spirit. Until then, as long as we are focused on Christ's completed work and the truth that all things testify to His glory, it's very difficult to wander far off course.

---

[131] Ephesians 4:16, 1 Corinthians 14:26
[132] Revelation 19:10

There will always be those who falsely claim to have the revelation of God, yet even here we have the Spirit's discernment. Once again, those who desire to protect their own doctrines will discourage people from heeding the Spirit within them. There will be times when you'll hear something taught and in your heart you'll feel the Spirit warning against it. Some call it a check in their spirit. It's the alert that something or someone is not in agreement with the truth of God.

I'll give an example. When I was doing some interim preaching, the church invited a preacher to speak who would potentially become their pastor. I had never met the man before and when I did meet him, I felt alarms going off in my spirit. I walked in the room where he sat and felt it before I even saw him. I looked over and he gave me a cold stare. I politely greeted him and he introduced himself as a potential pastor. From that point on, he was hostile toward me. Once he transitioned into that position, I and my family stepped away from the church. I had nothing specific to point to, so it was a delicate situation where I tried to say the right thing without looking like I didn't want to be replaced.

A few months later, he was asked to leave the church. His true colors were revealed. Many people left the church and much damage was done before he was removed.

Similar things have happened on several occasions. How could I possibly know this man was going to be an opposition to God without ever hearing a word or seeing any actions on his part? I couldn't know, but something in my spirit felt the opposition to the Holy Spirit and I knew intuitively that problems were brewing. As an interim, I could encourage leadership to seek the Lord's guidance, but had no authority to stop the coming storm.

Of course, there are many people who claim to have discernment and use it to attack others. This also is unbiblical, for a Christian is commanded to express the love of God to both enemies and brethren. The point is that when we feel a check in our spirit, we should stop and evaluate whether we are being alerted by the Spirit concerning false teaching or some other type of deception. When the Holy Spirit affirms truth to us, we should learn how to evaluate it against the scriptures and trust in the knowledge that comes from God and not bind ourselves by looking only to men for understanding.

You will never discover the deep things of the Spirit without learning how to listen to the Spirit. Look expectantly to God as you read the word, meditate on it, and spend time in prayer. Understanding is not only for the leaders of the church. We all have the anointing and knowledge of God. As we learn how to put our minds on the things of the Spirit, we will begin receiving understanding from the Spirit. The spiritually focused mind will begin receiving understanding from the Spirit. And as we appropriate what we are receiving, it will grow us into spiritual maturity and will become the foundation for the next truth God reveals to us.

Never will there be a time when God is not revealing deeper truths to us. We are only limited when we focus on the flesh or fall into the mindset that we have already learned it all, and stop seeking. The one who seeks finds. An expectant heart of faith will always receive from God.

Let's begin our conclusion of this book by reviewing **Hebrews 11:6**

> But without faith *it is* impossible to please *Him*, for he who comes to God must believe that He is, and *that* He is a rewarder of those who diligently seek Him.

All things are yours. Christ has completed the work and offers everything He accomplished to you as a free gift of His grace. The Christian life is not about what we do for God. The Christian life is about receiving the love of God. We seek because there is so much to this new life yet to be discovered. God rewards those who receive, because He gives to any who will seek, and then rewards us for possessing what He has given.

Faith is trusting in the completed work of Christ. Believe that God is who He said He is. Believe He has done what He said He has done. Then believe He loves you as much as He says He loves. Look at how much God loves you per Jesus' words in **John 17:23**

> I in them, and You in Me; that they may be made perfect in one, and that the world may know that You have sent Me, and have loved them as You have loved Me.

Did you catch that last phrase in this passage? God loves you as much as He does Christ. Because you are in Christ, you are in the fullness of God's love. And God loves you just as much as He loves Christ. If God loves you this much, how will He not give you all things? God expressed His love to you by first covering your sin, and then giving you His Spirit, and through that Spirit, God is drawing you to receive everything pertaining to life and godliness.

You lack nothing. Only believe in God's unstoppable love. Don't believe sin. Don't believe the accuser who throws guilt and condemnation in your face. Believe God. Then walk in the same Spirit you have been born into. When the flesh drags you down, simply get up, turn back to faith, and walk in victory. No groveling. No guilt. No shame. Trust in God's declaration that you are complete in Christ and live by faith in that proclamation. Then nothing can prevent you from receiving all that God has given.

The only thing God requires is faith – your trust in what He has done for you and provided to you. Anything you bring into faith that He has not provided is a work of the flesh.

Victory is already yours! Walk in it.

Discussion Questions:

Have you ever heard someone say, "God told me..." but then their actions proved otherwise?

Why do people think their thoughts are the words of God?

Can emotions mimic the affirmation of the Spirit?

What is the difference between faith in the flesh and faith that is based on the expectation of receiving from God?

Why does faith come by hearing the word of God?

Review Romans 8:7-9. If someone is walking according to their own understanding, but they are working in the church or doing ministry, can they please God? Why or why not?

Can teaching resources become a hindrance to what God is revealing to us? Explain.

Will we ever learn all God is revealing?

Read Ephesians 4:11-16. Does God make anyone independent of the body?

Does the church need every member?

Do we see this being practiced in our churches?

How does God prevent believers from wandering into error?

Why do people fall into errors and cultish ways of thinking?

How can we discern between our own displeasure and the discerning of the Holy Spirit?

Review 1 John 4:16-19. Why does the Bible tell us to believe in the love God has for us?

If we trust in His love, how does that affect our trust in His promises?

What does the Christian lack? What about you, do you lack anything?

How does knowing you already have been given all things affect how you approach the Christian life?

If you enjoyed this book, please rate it on Amazon.com.

You may also find encouragement in these titles by Eddie Snipes:
- The Victorious Christian Life: Living in Grace and Walking in the Spirit.
- The Promise of a Sound Mind : God's plan for emotional and mental health
- Simple Faith: How every person can experience intimacy with God
- I Called Him Dancer – Christian Fiction
- God Loves the Addict: Experiencing Recovery on the Path of Grace